D0411362

THE FIRST MUNROIST

AER as a young man in a loden wettermantel and woollen puttees.

THE FIRST MUNROIST

The Reverend A E Robertson: His Life,
Munros and Photographs

by Peter Drummond and Ian Mitchell

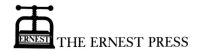

THE ERNEST PRESS

Published by The Ernest Press 1993
© Peter Drummond and Ian Mitchell

ISBN 0 948153 19 9

British Library Cataloguing-in-Publication Data
A catalogue record for this book is available from the British Library

Typeset in Ehrhardt 10 on 13pt by Edward M. Skelly, Berwick on Tweed

CONTENTS

Acknowledgements

The authors would like to thank the following people for their help in preparing this book.

Mrs Maud Tiso of Edinburgh for allowing us access to view the extensive collection of AER's slides held on behalf of the SMC by her late husband Graham Tiso.
Mrs Judith Lewis of Edinburgh, Secretary of the Scottish Rights of Way Society, for allowing us access to their records and assisting us in our search.
The SMC Secretary John R R Fowler for allowing us access to AER's hillwalking logs and his collection of diaries. Also for allowing reproduction of AER's slides.
The Reverend Archibald Chisholm, Mr Archibald Campbell, and Mr Ward-Campbell, all of Rannoch parish in Perthshire, for help within AER's old parish.
Mrs J D B Wilson of Dunblane for her gift of her late husband's collection of SMC Journals, which covered the period of AER's activities.
Mrs Elizabeth Stevenson of Dunblane, Mrs Elspet MacKay of Edinburgh and Mrs Mary Clarkson of Edinburgh for their memories of Winifred Hutchison, AER's second wife.
Kate Whitley of the Ladies' Scottish Climbing Club for locating old articles by Winifred Robertson.
Mrs Lind of Edinburgh for allowing us access to AER's former residence to take photos of his craftsmanship.
Hamish Brown of Fife for his information.
Gordon McGavin of Larkhall for his advice on old cameras.
Ken Crocket, editor of the Scottish Mountaineering Club Journal, for permission to quote from the Journals.
Les Jenkins of Lenzie for his proof-reading work.
Peter Hodgkiss our publisher for his encouragement, advice and malt whisky.
Ian Allan of Coatbridge for assistance with maps.
Bob Aitken for information.

Glossary of Abbreviations used.

AER	– Archibald Eneas Robertson
BD	– Bachelor of Divinity, a Scottish theological qualification
CCJ	– Cairngorm Club Journal
CIC	– (Hut). The Charles Inglis Clark memorial hut on Ben Nevis
GD	– reference number of Scottish Rights of Way Society files in Scottish Records Office
LSCC	– Ladies Scottish Climbing Club
MA	– Master of Arts, a Scottish university degree
SMC	– Scottish Mountaineering Club
SMCJ	– Scottish Mountaineering Club Journal. (The number appearing after this abbreviation refers to the volume of the journal – eg SMCJ 7, p10.)

Illustrations

Foreword

by John Smith, Q.C., M.P.

A few days after my friend and constituent Peter Drummond asked me to write a foreword to this book, I climbed Beinn Chaluim. It was a cold winter's day and as we gathered at Kirkton Farm the frost was hard on the ground and the cloud hung over the hill. As I laced up my boots I thought to myself that while I was determined to get to the top, this might be one of the many similar outings on which I saw very little from the summit. How wrong I was. About 1000 feet up we broke through the cloud inversion and entered a magical world. The sky was blue, the sunlight reflected on the snow, and above an all-encompassing sea of cloud all we could see in every direction was mountains.

To the south the Crianlarich Hills and the Arrochar Alps, to the east the Lawers group, to the west Cruachan, and to the north and north-west Ben Nevis itself and the Mamlorn hills. I do not believe there was a better place to be on the face of the earth that winter's day than on the top of a Scottish mountain.

Although I was born in the shadow of Cruachan, I only came to mountaineering late in life. But I cannot adequately express the enjoyment I have had from the experience. Climbing the hills as a conscious recreation is only a hundred years old but I am glad to say it is becoming ever more popular. All of us who enjoy the Scottish mountains owe a debt of gratitude to the redoubtable Sir Hugh who tabulated the Munros. But we also ought to pay our grateful respects to the first man to climb them all, and who is the subject of this fascinating biography, the Reverend A E Robertson. Had he not pioneered the ascent of all the Munros – I hesitate to attach the slightly pejorative description of "the first Munro-bagger" to a Victorian divine – would others have followed in his path? Would Scottish mountaineering have become the popular and fast-growing sport that it has undoubtedly become today?

In this highly readable book we join AER in his pilgrimage: we share his experience of people and places; we enjoy his idiosyncratic observations; we learn part of the fascinating history of Scottish mountaineering.

It will be read with pleasure by all those who, like AER, love the hills of Scotland.

Part One: The Man

CHAPTER ONE

The Munro-bagging pilgrimage

In late September 1901 three figures approach the small cairn on the summit of Meall Dearg above Glen Coe. Only a few score of boots have stood there before. But this is a very special day for the mountain and for the three individuals – a minister, his wife and his lawyer friend. For the minister is about to find his holy grail – the final summit in his pilgrimage up and down all the Munros.

Munro-bagging can be like a religious pilgrimage. The pleasure of arrival is greater if chafed by the sackcloth of hard travelling. The more penitential the journey has been, the sweeter the attainment of the last summit. How fitting then that today's legions of born-again Munro-baggers seek to follow in the footsteps of a man of the cloth, the Reverend A E Robertson.

Faith is an essential quality for Munro-bagging. How else can one suffer, for instance, the pushing of the flesh up the featureless contours of Carn na Caim in a pervasive drizzle? Sir Hugh Munro, compiler of the holy writ of the Munro Tables, may have a lot to answer for as father of the idea on such soul-searching occasions, but in AER he had a minister on Earth, a Columbus who demonstrated that it could be done.

Messianic zeal was not obvious throughout the Reverend Robertson's campaign however, for he took over a decade to cover the 283 peaks then inscribed in the Tables. He himself was to write that the campaign 'has been a desultory one, and has occupied about ten years.' Indeed:

> It was begun with no thought of ever climbing them all, but simply from a desire to obtain a general knowledge of the Highland hills.' (SMCJ 7, p10)

His first Munro was Cruachan which he climbed in 1889, and in the ensuing years he clocked up a steady if modest annual total. But it was nearly nine years into his decade of Munro-bagging – in 1898 – before he began to display the fervour of the convert: up until then he had climbed about a hundred summits, but 1898 and 1899 saw two grand walking tours in the Highlands which netted nearly 150 new summits between them and left but a couple of dozen to complete. His sudden burst of zeal is all the more striking because it came after a hill-walking doldrums of two years which saw very few peaks, the summer of 1897 being spent indeed on golf courses, atop cycle saddles, and at whist evenings – amongst sinners, so to speak!

The location of his Damascus conversion may well lie on a foreign summit. In the early spring of 1898 he went on holiday to Italy, of which his diary records few details other than that on March 4th he climbed Vesuvius – for the second time in three days. Vesuvius was not really an exciting mountain in itself – they rode on horses to the foot and climbed up the ashy cone – its height being nearly on eyeball terms with Ben Nevis, and it has a funicular railway, built by Thomas Cook in 1880, depositing large numbers of vulgar trippers on top. But it must have had the romantic aura of foreign parts with the added spice of the intriguing thought that you and the volcano could be blown off the face of the earth at any moment.

It is a common experience of Scots going abroad to the higher mountains of Europe or Asia that they see the hills of home in a new light on return, appreciating them and their qualities in a new way. Perhaps this soft focus effect sharpened to become the vision that was to light up the arduous path ahead over the remaining Munros and to provide the reflected gleam in his eyes as he strode up to yet another cairn in the next two years. His European tour continued for another month with but desultory entries in his diary, via Milan, Paris and London, arriving home in April. So he had scarcely shaken the lava dust off his boots when he was crunching up to the snowy top of Aonach Mor on the second day of May. There he stood panning round the northern horizon, from Knoydart to the Cairngorms and beyond, scanning what was to be the stage for his many-peaked pilgrimage of that summer.

And it was a pilgrimage in which the flame of the convert's passion burned fiercely. For the first time in his diaries we find the imprecation 'bagged' called down upon a peak (on A'Ghlas Bheinn, a fine peak deserving a more respectful term). Even the death of his mother at the start of June, when a telegram recalled him from Torridon, interrupted his peak-collecting for less than the week it took him to journey home, bury her, return to Achnasheen and the next day to An Coileachan, the start of a further six weeks in the hills. The frenetic pace reached was indicated by his log's admission that 'I bagged Moruisg (3026 feet) between trains' while travelling between Balmacara and Grantown-on-Spey!

The missionary fire, whose jet had so suddenly burst into life in the spring of 1898, seemed nevertheless to drop to a mere peep in the autumn of 1899 at the end of that next summer's odyssey of 72 peaks. For from the July day in 1899 when his boots stepped off the yielding surfaces of Sgairneach Mhor onto the metalled road to Perth (and with but two dozen or so peaks still to conquer for the cause), until Easter 1901 when he wielded an ice-axe on Beinn a'Chroin to cut the steps that led symbolically onto the steep but short few months to his last peak in September ... in that twenty-month spell between these two hills he climbed but one or two Munros. Why was this? Surely his marriage to Kate in August 1900 had not turned the mountain goat into a glen mouse, or put a domestic lampshade over the light of his ambition? Or was he slightly ashamed of the apparent unseemliness of his rush to complete the round in a Club (the Scottish Mountaineering Club) where '... Peak-bagging and record-breaking are, I fear, somewhat looked down upon...'. It was after all a Club in which he was still a 'young upstart' with few climbing achievements or Journal articles to his credit. Whatever the reason he must have burned with frustration at being so near and yet so far from consummating the achievement, if his 1902 article in the SMCJ is accurate when he says that:

> ... for many years past the writer has very much wanted to kiss every summit that finds a place in the historic 'Tables'. (op. cit.)

And perhaps the pent-up frustration was also responsible for the unhappy turn of phrase he uses to describe reaching his particular Jerusalem, Meall Dearg on the Aonach Eagach ridge, at the second or third attempt:

... after many vicissitudes and exertions at length, last September (1901), in Glencoe, I **wiped out** the last of the 3000 footers ... (our emphasis) (op. cit.)

Or did he? Suggestions have been made that AER did not in fact complete all the Munros. Of course, in a 'collection' where the only proof of complete ownership is a man's word that he has been to all the summits, such a suggestion could be hung on the hatstands of many of the listed compleaters. Indeed the officially published Munro list refers to 'claims' of completion, a nice legal term. And in the Reverend's case there are little clouds over two of his peaks.

One is Ben Wyvis, that great beached whale of a flat-topped hill in Easter Ross. His log, written retrospectively a decade later, says that in August 1892 (early in his hill career):

I did B. Wyvis, taking train to Auchterneed from Tain. I followed the usual way up but near the top it came on heavy rain and as I did not want to get soaked I turned.

There is no other record either in his personal diaries (a very brief set of entries, often incomplete and certainly not systematic) or in his Log (written retrospectively) of a second ascent of this hill. This does not rule out the possibility that he did return, for his records were not too thorough. And since he returned to other nearly-done peaks elsewhere near the end of his completion, to 'tidy up' loose ends – indeed his final peak Meall Dearg was one such – does this not suggest that he would not have omitted this one, had it been still

incomplete? But if he did not, then one is left wrestling with thorny moral problems. How 'near the top' do you have to be to be on top? Or – since the 'usual way up' he describes is a plod from Strathpeffer a lot longer and duller than today's *voie normale* – could we count it as a Munro awarded for effort, a victory on points if not by knockout? How many angels could dance on the point of the Wyvis cairn? And did Saint Peter have it ticked off for him in his Tables? We shall never know.

The other clouded peak, and **definitely** undone in September 1901, was the famous Inaccessible Pinnacle in Skye. He could, of course, if challenged at the Pearly Gates on this one, answer truthfully that at that time it was not a full Munro in the Tables, merely a top. Only in 1921 did it swap status with the adjacent summit of Sgurr Dearg, in a revision of the Tables. In the original Tables, as well as to the naked eye, the Pinnacle was clearly higher than the Dearg top (3250 feet and 3234 feet respectively), but perhaps Munro felt that, as it is a flake of rock like a shark's fin, it was not organically the summit of the mountain, more of a wart-like excrescence. AER could not himself be blamed for this curious definition of geological reality, and could legitimately claim the official summit in the Tables.

However he does appear to have done the Pinnacle some years later, and certainly long before the second compleater the Reverend A R G Burn in 1923. He took a photo of the Pinnacle in summer 1906 while there with a party of competent climbers including MacRobert, and may well have climbed it then, for he took up rock-climbing after his Munro completion. Even more surely he climbed it in 1908, shortly before his one and only trip to the Alps, for which it would have been acceptable training. In the SMC Journal for

The Inaccessible Pinnacle

January 1909, Francis Greig writes in his article *Midsummer Days in the Cuillin* about '... a large party headed by the Reverend A E Robertson bound for the Inaccessible Pinnacle hove into sight 500 feet above us ...'. A later Note, unattributed, in the same edition reveals that the 'large party' consisted of six – AER himself, Rory MacKenzie (nephew of the famous guide

John), two ladies Mrs D Urquhart and Miss Lowson, with G Gibbs and K Watson – and that they first traversed Sgurr a'Mhadaidh. The latter three headed for Bidein Druim nan Ramh while:

> The remaining members of the party traversed the Inaccessible from east to west (SMCJ 10, p225)

No moral problems with this one! And he was ahead of many modern Munroists in that he seems to have made this ascent of the Pinnacle without difficulty, not having to be hauled up in undignified style like some (indeed like the Rev. Burn himself), nor being unable to fully complete the Munros because of this one rock barrier. What price the putative few metres of gently rising contours on Wyvis, when he could so ably ice the cake by traversing this airy height on Sgurr Dearg? Let us return to join him on the other Dearg, the equally spectacular summit of Glen Coe's Meall Dearg where he completed the official round of the Munros and fulfilled his vision.

The spark from Vesuvius that, three years earlier, had set alight his still-smouldering vision was to be drowned at this cairn in glasses of champagne for the completed campaign. A card was inscribed with details of the achievement, placed in the empty bottle and inserted into the cairn. It lay there for several decades, being examined by Lord Strathcona and a keeper in 1930: and AER himself wrote in the 1950 SMC Journal that this bottle 'was to be found until recently hidden in the cairn.' Since they had consumed a quart (over a litre) of Ayala champagne between three of them, they must have fairly skipped and giggled down the hill. AER's own log confesses:

Schiehallion Summit

> We descended the steep scree gully with ease!! I at
> any rate never descended a scree slope with less
> trouble! The screes melted away under my
> feet ... Such is the effect of much champagne!!
> (Log, 2, p28)

But what remained after the bubbly's effervescence
was, paradoxically, something more spiritual yet longer-
lasting – the establishment of a path to all the Munros
had been beaten not on the very slopes but in the
imagination of future generations. The customs of
modern compleaters toasting their own success on the
final summit is but an echo of the clink of these raised
glasses on Meall Dearg.

CHAPTER TWO

Bens and Glens

At the Scottish Mountaineering Club's Jubilee dinner in 1938, the Reverend Robertson proposed the traditional toast to 'The Bens and Glens'. One member present, the celebrated climber J H B Bell, was to write years later in the SMC Journal's obituary for AER that no-one there could ever forget the 'vivid brilliance and feeling' with which he had proposed it in '... a speech (or was it an incantation) of 3 minutes duration.' One can almost hear the ministerial intonation sound across the years as the Reverend declaimed this hymn to the Highlands. And he would have meant every word about both the bens and the glens, for he was never a mere Munro-bagger but a treader of hills of all sizes and a stravaiger of the low roads too. He was also a rock-climber and, throughout his career, a path explorer. He climbed abroad, if only twice – Vesuvius in 1898 and the Matterhorn and Rimpfischhorn in 1908 – and on lesser hills like the Lomonds of Fife and Norman's Law (not even 1000 feet, but he recorded his appreciation of a 'good view'), and Edinburgh's Pentlands and Arthur's Seat, as well as Arran's Corbetts. All hill life was his, from Alpine peaks through Munros and sub-Donalds down to bealachs!

And he began his hill adventures, as so many do, on lower peaks, the Arran Donalds. The young Archibald Aeneas may well have been a solitary (as well as an only) child, and his first hill experiences were undertaken alone. As a boy of 12 or 13 in 1882 or 1883 (he himself wasn't quite sure), going off from his holiday home in

Zermatt and Matterhorn

the manse at Brodick, he wandered first over the Saddle between Glen Sannox and Glen Rosa, and then made a solo ascent of Goat Fell, Arran's highest peak. Many West of Scotland youngsters have their first taste of the hills here, but not many do it alone as he did, nor choose the sporting route to the top leaving the path at 2000 feet '... and going straight up the slope, finding great delight in scrambling over the boulders, so steeply set.'

The sharp taste of adrenalin savoured that day – he reinforced it by descending the same way – would be recalled from the body's memory many times in adulthood, but among the butterfly experiences of childhood it was to lie chrysalis-like until 1889 and the verge of manhood. Then he stayed in a family-rented holiday home on Loch Awe and one day rowed over the loch, this time with other lads, to climb Cruachan. Here occurred an odd incident, with Arran connections: a stranger approached them and asked if he could join them. Though seemingly an innocent request, the young men's minds were full of images of the recent murder-by-pushing of a Mr Rose on Goat Fell committed by an unknown assailant (later named as a Mr Lawrie), who was still on the loose and '... we boys were much suspicious that the stranger was he!' After a huddle of whispers and sidelong glances he was allowed to join them, and turned out to be an Edinburgh schools inspector, an inspirer of fear only in the minds of cowed pupils. They climbed Cruachan but AER could not remember much of the trip or even whether they actually had a view on top, the memory perhaps wiped by the edgy encounter with the suspected shover.

By contrast the following summer his ascent of the Devil's Staircase was in company amongst whom a young man of breeding felt more relaxed – two doctors, a minister and an advocate. He patently admired not only the view of Rannoch and 'the chain of the Blackwater lochs' (the dam not being built until 1905), but also the erudition of his mentors. His log, in rather simpering style, records his admiration of Mr Innis' geological knowledge, and the Reverend Thomson's

'apt and beautiful' lines of poetry recited as they rode along Loch Leven. He wrote that on that day '... my love for the hills was generated', and as with many hill-goers since, the presence of a social company that he felt at ease with would have imparted a rosy glow to the hills. The ascent of the Devil's Staircase is after all hardly a feast of hill-walking excitement: the men as much as the mountains, the people as much as the peaks, are and were the link between individual climbers and the hills.

He quickly established his credentials with this desirable social group by making a solo ascent of Ben Nevis, taking tea in the mist-smored summit café, and soon after was invited to join another party of gentlemen in the ascent of Bidean nam Bian. This party contained yet another amateur geologist, a Mr Peyton – the study of rocks was deemed Victorian justification for the seeming frivolity of climbing them. He seems to have accompanied the party in the erratic manner of an energetic dog for '... he skipped about with his hammer, peering here and there, whacking this, tearing at that,

Bidean nam Bian: September 1928

never still'. Morality was never far from the surface, Mr Peyton being 'much scandalised' at another of the party whose ascent was apparently aided by frequent sips of rum, and he lectured another upon discovering that he had no nails on his boots, intoning that to climb without '... adds 1000 feet to a hill'. The wide-eyed apprentice Aeneas recorded this maxim '... which I have never forgotten.'

The Bidean day nearly ended still more unforgettably when a large rock was dislodged by Dr Whyte while above the party at a point when it was positioned randomly across a scree face. It nearly ended Mr Peyton's interest in stones of all sizes (including the small ones he was shaking out of one boot at the time) and he, oblivious to the ironic possibilities of a geologist being whacked by a rock, phlegmatically muttered another maxim 'That was a near thing'.

Little else of note occurred on this day, memorable for AER alone because it was his first taste of big hills shared with companions and spiced with adventure. Most mountaineers and Munro-baggers since have clear memories of a day early in their montane careers when the spirit of the hills came upon them, when trivia seem titanic and boulders become beinns. This was his day of dawning.

The day ended with the apprentice lugging along a bag of rocks for the geologist, but the load must have felt light to our young man of springing step who had just experienced '... the delights of scientific mountaineering (the use of maps, aneroid, compass) ... since that day I have steadily pursued that quest.' The Victorian era, then in its heyday, was underpinned by the philosophy of man's triumph over Nature through scientific progress and the spirit of adventure, and the concept of 'scientific mountaineering' was to provide a fine banner to fly in his pilgrimage through the hills. That, and the companionship of a band of social equals and superiors in what was then very much an elite sport for gentlemen, kept his eye on the far blue horizon.

And so it was that his next encounter with the Scottish hills – two summers on after a spell in America and immediately after graduating – was again in the company of a gentleman, specifically a Mr Somerville who invited him to spend a week at Aviemore, some decades before commercialism altered the tone of this Victorian watering hole. They climbed Braeriach on a clear and lovely day when '... I had my taste for scientific mountaineering deepened and confirmed' by the use of Mr Somerville's map, compass and aneroid which '... greatly charmed me.' On top they encountered more gentlemen whose gait, gear and general knowledge of surrounding peaks marked them apart from mere tourists. One of them turned out to be William Douglas, editor of the SMC Journal. A short walk, a talk, an exchange of calling cards and AER was left an apostle of the new creed of Scottish mountaineering. The new-kindled fire survived the next day through a quenching downpour, gale and mist on Cairn Gorm where some rather unscientific mountaineering (he forgot to allow for magnetic variation in the compass) got him and his companion lost.

Another habit, given the stamp of authority by the high priests on Braeriach, was to stay with him over the years. William Douglas and his companion had '... helped us greatly in identifying the view', and AER obviously took this to be the done thing, a genuflection at the summit as at a station of the cross. It would of course be in line with the Victorian ethos of scientific description, to give detail of the view and of which peaks could be seen from another. Thus his journal contains such rivetting verbal panoramas as this one from atop Geal Charn (above Loch Pattack) after he had built its first cairn, written from notes made on the spot:

> View north **obstructed** by Creag Meagaidh. Ben Nevis, fine knobbly top. Long ridge of Aonachs. Serrated peaks of Binnein Mor and Sgor a'Mhaim. Schiehallion **not seen** because of Ben Alder. Flat ridge of Clachlet. Long flat range of Glen Lyon hills. Ben Dorain, Achallader rising sharply. Cruachan **not seen** because of haze. Sugarloaf-like cones of the Buachailles. (Our emphases) (Log 1, p15)

Eat your heart out, stout Cortez, for even your eagle eyes could not pick up the peaks you could **not** see because of obstructions! Of course Victorians like the Reverend felt themselves to be striding the world in step with the great explorers, recounting every blink of a new land. This also accounts for the obsession with the time of ascents. For instance the previous day he logged the time of 11.05 at Loch Ericht Lodge, a departure off the path at 1.50, an arrival at Ben Alder's summit at 3 o'clock and a departure therefrom at 3.20. The distant chugging of an engine on the railway then being built across Rannoch Moor would have set the timetabling tone of his records.

This 1893 walk, his first major expedition under his own steam, was preceded by the laying-in of the necessary equipment. That spring he had become the proud owner of a 'rücksack' (still spelt with the German Umlaut as its newness prevented English accepting it

Snow tunnel north of Rannoch Station, July 1924

yet), and an ice-axe from the Chamonix maker Simond at a total cost including postage of a guinea. He obtained a London-made aneroid at almost three times that price (£3) via his old mentor Lord Kelvin: the master's specification was so good that the instrument survived AER and was presented by his widow to the SMC nearly seventy years on. He bought a pair of boots – '... my old hobnailers' – from Wrights of Edinburgh, that lasted into 1898, and a compass (from Whites of Glasgow). The first two of all these items, he tells us, went with him on his first big walking tour in 1893. A few eyebrows must have been raised and smiles suppressed at this fresh-faced young man striding forth 'alpenstock in hand' ... in early July!

The spring of that year had seen him try out this new toy, the ice-axe, on the peaks near Dalmally in company with fellow-students. Hair-raising adventures including a near-disastrous day on Ben Lui (when he nearly went through a cornice) perhaps suggest a divine protecting hand cupped around his youthful blunders! Most young beginners on the winter hills have had similar near-misses and heart-pumping happenings, and AER was no exception in learning fast from what nearly came to pass. Thus, the following winter saw his ice-axe put to safer and more disciplined use on his first serious winter climb with the SMC on Ben Lui, learning at the blunt end of Tough's rope.

The ice-axe was to figure in his only other conscious brush with death in the hills, twelve years later in April 1905. He was descending a snow-gully on Ben Nevis in a blizzard and thunderstorm, when he was struck by lightning, probably through this ice-axe. He regained consciousness a couple of thousand feet lower than memory had last placed him, lacerated and burnt about the face and head. With torn garments he staggered down to Fort William where a doctor was summoned to insert twenty stitches in his head. His diary anxiously noted that his body temperature was one degree below

Ben Nevis Observatory

normal that evening, and he took a day or two to recover. His ice-axe, the probable attraction for the thunderbolt, had been lost on the Ben along with his cap, but fortunately not his life. The incident was sufficiently notable to be recorded for posterity in the book *Twenty Years on Ben Nevis*, a record of the experiences of the famous mist-clad mountain-top observatory there. How he managed to stagger to his Fort William hotel was, in the words of author William Kilgour '... almost as great a mystery as his marvellous escape from death.'

The mists of spring 1894 in the Grampians were the test for his first serious navigation using map, compass and aneroid in '... the longest and most intricate piece of steering I have ever done' which he passed with flying colours to emerge '... just where we expected' (ie, at the top of the class!) even if thoroughly soaked.

Technique developed and equipment amassed, he was ready for his first full love affair with a particular hill, and it came in the Cairngorms that summer of 1894. Three months were spent at Coylumbridge in a genteel Victorian round of visits, dinners, picnics, walks and occasional forays to the tops. Of ten days spent on the summits, five including the first and the last were devoted to the soft contours of Braeriach. How many of today's single-minded Munro-baggers would contemplate such devotion to one hill? Mind you, like so many first loves, it seems to have been phased out of later memory, and no picture of Braeriach alone can be found in the Reverend's later photo albums!

In the mid-1890s his gradual accumulation of Munros, mainly at the SMC's New Year and Easter meets and in his 1895 summer walking tour, was interspersed by relaxation in the glens and by the lochs, cycling (another of his life-long passions) and trout-fishing (for a month at Kenmore).

Then came his conversion on the road to Damascus (somewhere near Vesuvius) which ushered in the two-year love-blind spell when Munro-bagging was all he could see in the hills, leading on via his two big walks of 1898 and 1899 (chapter 4), to the eventual completion in 1901. In his 1902 article in the SMCJ summing up the campaign he spoke of his plans for the future, and declared his undying love for the Munros thus:

> ... in answer to silly people who ask me 'What will you do now since you have no more worlds to conquer?' I can only say, 'I am going to climb them all over again'. (SMCJ 7, p14)

Romantic yes, but accurate no! For, after his completion of the Munros, there is little evidence of him trying to climb them all again. His interests in the hills were starting to change again.

Some areas, like the Cuillin of Skye, were revisited many times in the years to follow, while others scarcely saw his boots again. The proof of this lies not only in his diaries but also from the lens of his camera. He took up photography only after he had completed the round of the Munros. But there is hardly a photograph amongst his voluminous work thereafter of the Cairngorms, the Grampians and the Southern Highlands. His photos reflect his hill interests in the 20th century, and they are mainly of Skye, the Western Highlands and Lochaber.

The first decade of the new century also saw him indulge in rock-climbing, especially from 1903 to 1906 (see Chapter 6), and he began to take a more relaxed view of his old flames, the Munro summits, with photography often being the excuse for not making the date. Thus at the Easter 1909 meet he did climb Ben Nevis on the first day, but as the Journal records he and three other members:

> ... sauntered up the Allt a'Mhuilinn, photographing as they went, climbed to the top of the Carn Mor Dearg arête and so to the top of Ben Nevis. (SMCJ 10, p337)

The following day he and six others '... took a day off to visit the aluminium works at Kinlochleven.'! Even the summits revisited were secondary to the new love of photography. The Easter 1908 meet was thus recorded in the SMC Journal:

Castle Ridge, April 1928.

On Monday Workman, MacRobert and the two Youngs ascended the maze of steps in the Ben Lui corrie and, nearing the summit, were subjected to a rapid fire from that keen photographer A E Robertson who had already ascended by the Fox's Couloir. (op. cit. p134)

The camera indeed was more of an encumbrance than an aid to climbing. Being a plate camera on a tripod, it would have been quite heavy and clumsy. One account of a summer hill day in 1906 by G Bennet Gibbs, whose party met up with the Reverend's party in Glencoe, writes that:

> The 'Meenister' would have photographed parts of the climb had not the rain-clouds descending on the hills made the good work impossible, not to mention the difficulty of getting baggage through the first section – the service as yet not being open for Parcels Post – and with five climbers on 160 feet of rope, there was none to spare for hauling; so the 'bagpipes' – as the camera in a sack with short legs protruding was nicknamed – had to be left at the foot of the rocks with other impedimenta, to be called for on the return. (SMCJ 9, p16)

Camera tripods and their legs kept getting in his way, so to speak. An account of the Easter 1909 Meet spoke of:

> The Meenister was in evidence on Friday generously carrying some spare legs over the hill in case any one found their normal number insufficient for the task. (SMCJ 10, p274)

Increasingly as the 20th century bedded in, the demands of the dog collar chained him to the glens rather than the bens. He was appointed minister in charge of the Braes of Rannoch parish in late 1906, taking up his duties in 1907. The 1909 account just quoted continues:

> The folk of the town were relieved to see him leave on Saturday afternoon for his own parish – 'far up tae muir among the heather' – not so those visitors who would gladly have sat under him. (op. cit.)

In spite of this new posting 'among the heather' he continued attending SMC New Year and Easter Meets for a while, but then vanished into obscurity for a lengthy period. He never appeared at a single SMC Meet between 1910 and 1925. Even outwith the club, hills appear to recede, in his personal diaries, into the far blue yonder for a decade and a half, until rapid elevation within the heirarchy of the Scottish Mountaineering Club provided a springboard for a renewed relationship with the bens and glens.

1906 SMC meet at Clachaig, showing some of AER's companions – seated bottom left is J A Parker; 4th from left is G B Gibbs; squatting 7th from left is Wm Douglas; and next is W W Naismith with Raeburn's camera resting on his head; A E Maylard is stood next to Raeburn; a smiling F S Goggs is stood 5th from right.

CHAPTER THREE

The Scottish Mountaineering Club

Glen Affric Meet, Easter 1932. AER is 3rd from right standing: P J H Unna is at far left.

AER's relationship with the Scottish Mountaineering Club (the SMC) seemed to blow hot and cold, with periods of intense activity punctuated by long absences. One of their earliest members, he outlasted many of the pioneers, and scaled the Club's contours from the humble post of Slide Custodian to the pinnacle of Presidency.

He joined enthusiastically in 1893, with his application signed by Professor Ramsay and William Douglas (SMC Journal Editor), and listing his hills climbed to date (45 Munros at that point). His membership was approved at the Club's 5th AGM that December, and he himself was present to celebrate at the Club Dinner that evening as his latter proposer's guest. By the time he went on his first Club Meet a fortnight later he had already penned his first journal article, on the Creag Meagaidh range. This must have given him great delight as he held the Journal in high regard, being as it was a pioneering publication in more senses than one. His own journal years later recalled:

> Some time early in the winter of 1892 Mr Somerville gave me the SMC Journal no. 6 which I read eagerly. I soon afterwards bought all the previous numbers up. They were still in print and cost me 1/- each except no. 1 for which I paid 2/6d. (Log 1, opposite p7)

This first Meet for him, 1894's New Year at Dalmally, 'every hour of which I enjoyed', saw him throw himself into his first real snow and ice work, and in the first flush of enthusiasm he attended almost all of the bi-annual Meets for the next two years, at New Year and Easter, his exploits there being recorded in the Journal's despatches ... Thus at his first Meet he climbed with Burnett and the aptly-named Tough on the north-east face of Ben Lui, and 'learned much' from the latter's skill and guidance. Exactly one year later to the day he experienced another testing snow and ice day, a traverse on the Cobbler in the company of such great names as Naismith and Maylard.

However, he does not seem to have made much development as an ice climber, and at the next two Meets seemed happier hill-walking. Indeed the Journal of 1896 notes that, on the New Year Meet's Thursday:

> Moncrieff and Robertson bagged Beinn Chaluim. Of their adventures nothing is recorded further than that they went up the hill and came down again. As this particular hill exceeds 3000 feet, its ascent therefore comes in the shape of a duty to the conscientious peak-bagger. (SMCJ 4, p127)

14

(Note the prophetic, or perhaps ironic, last sentence!)

Now while AER clearly revelled in the clubbable atmosphere of these Meets, of mountain days and smoking-room nights, perhaps he realised that his hill-walking inclinations didn't quite match the more serious aspirations of the majority on Meets. The Club was divided into Ultramontanes (whose goal was to achieve the scaling of all manner of difficult rock and ice) and the Salvationists, for whom the evening's safe return to the glen was paramount. Salvationism was an acceptable tendency, with respectable adherents like the great Sir Hugh Munro himself, but most of them were probably under pressure to do some of the hard stuff too at Meets. On the other hand, perhaps his new job as assistant minister in Edinburgh precluded attendance at the New Year and Easter Meets. Whatever the reasons, he disappeared from these bi-annual gatherings for some six years, precisely at the time when his Munro-bagging activities were in full swing.

However, with the Munros completed in 1901, his eyes re-focused on new horizons and (as related in chapter 6) he turned to more serious rock-climbing activities in the first decade of the new 20th century. Parallel with this he returned to the SMC fold in 1902 and attended regularly all the way through until 1910, although participating mainly as a hill-walker and photographer. Off the hill, he was the Club's slide custodian from 1903 to 1906, and many of his articles on route description date from this period of involvement. But why did he no longer feel out of place alongside the serious rock and ice men? Probably because he had now 'proved himself' in another mountain sphere by climbing all the Munros, and so was not in need of justifying his gentler activities.

Summit of Bidein Druim nan Ramh.

However he had, in the six-year absence from official Meets, mixed with chosen members. For instance he spent part of June 1898 with Parker and the Inglis Clarks climbing and scrambling in the Cuillin. The SMC Journal records that '... after the departure of the others that inveterate 'peak-bagger' Robertson climbed Banachdich...'

He ended the first decade of the new century, his Club-active decade, by attending the 1910 Kinlochewe Meet (where his exploits were so timid as to be unrecorded) and then radio silence descends for fifteen years. He re-appears on the Journal's wavelength in 1925, at the Meets and at the AGM. At the New Year Meet he took lochside walks, and with Gilbert Thomson 'discussed the old days by the murmuring River Strae.' At the Easter Meet he obviously felt no reticence on account of returning after so many years' absence, for when he met the younger, outstanding climbers J H B Bell and Frank Smythe, he bluntly introduced himself, public school prefect-like, 'I'm Robertson. Who are you?'! At that year's AGM he gave the members 'a real treat' with a slide show of his own taking. The accompanying 'sound track' included what the Journal described as 'his inimitable Highland stories ... and his own delectable species of humour.' One of the stories was about Prince Charlie's Cave on Ben Alder supplied (he punned) with a spring mattress ... of the type that ensured fresh water!

The Reverend had a definite feeling for the Prince, later writing an article about his post-Culloden wanderings in the hills. And this was perhaps an outcrop of the subconscious through to the surface, for his return to Club activity was as sudden and dramatic as that of the exiled Prince two centuries before. He appeared (late) at the Easter 1927 Meet, bagging only the village of Kinlochleven during the weekend: and later that year at the AGM, after an effective absence of nearly two decades from the Club's activities on the hill,

Kinlochleven, April 1927.

raised his standard as Vice-President. Thus started a long reign first as Vice-President, then President from 1929 to 1932, and as General Editor of the Club's Guidebooks from 1931 to 1945. During most of this reign he felt it necessary to appear at Meets, missing none between 1928 and 1933, and still managing the 1938 New Year gathering at Crianlarich. In his late fifties at the start of this period and pushing seventy by Crianlarich, he confined himself to gentler walks, photographic expeditions, and indeed acted as chauffeur in his newly-acquired car to younger members who sought peaks more distant from the hotel base.

Even over two decades after his completion, there was still an air of mystery and a sense of exploration among club members attempting some of the remoter Munros, and they would turn to AER for advice. In 1927, for example, J A Parker (a leading member) was exploring the hills north of the Garve – Ullapool road, among which lies Seana Bhraigh. 'I wonder,' wrote Parker, 'how many members of the club have been on top of the hill or even seen it!' He continued, in the April 1928 SMCJ to say that 'All the information about it that I could get *from the leading authority in Edinburgh* (our emphases) on "separate mountains" was that it was a long distance from anywhere...' Not very detailed, but the Reverend, from his capital city home, could at least blame three decades of misted memory since his ascent.

As Club official, he may even have allowed flattery to overcome artistic taste when he featured in a breathtaking Club song, a feature of the 1929 Meets, designed to be sung in unison by all the splendid fellows and stout chaps there present. Here is a snatch of what other guests at the Alexandra Hotel, Fort William, might have heard wafting from the dining room:

> MacRobert and Robertson – they're a pair,
> Hurrah! Hurrah!
> Vice-presidents both – beyond compare,
> Hurrah, Hurrah!
> If they are our vices, you'll wonder with me
> Why! What in the world must our virtues be!
>
> (Chorus) Oh we all feel jolly well bucked to belong to the SMC,
> Oh we all feel jolly well bucked to belong to the SMC!'
> (SMCJ 18, p368)

He probably enjoyed still more the paterfamilias role into which he entered as President later that year, being at the centre of the Meets at least in the evenings, and advising the 'youngsters' on photography and on routes. He must have loved the Journal's glimpses of him, in this role, which paint a fond picture:

> The feature of the whole Meet was the arrival of Robertson in a kilt. The tartan, appropriately enough for such a well-known conqueror of peaks, was the Hunting Robertson (Killin, 1935) ... He was appropriately the last to haul down his flag, leaving at 12.30 (Arrochar, 1931) ... on New Year's Night a line of continuity with the last Meet held here (Dalmally) was forged by the arrival of the Reverend A E Robertson, who had also been present in 1894. (1936 Meet, Dalmally)

He also officiated, as 'house chaplain', at the 1929 opening of the CIC Hut. He called a blessing upon the hut, that it be a place of refuge in time of trouble, and

then they all sang the 121st Psalm ('I to the hills...'). As if in response to the benediction winging its way heavenward, later that evening two exhausted climbers stumbling glenward burst in on the official celebrations, dishevelled after a 600 feet slide down Observatory Gully. A cup of tea apparently sufficed to see them on their way down the Allt a'Mhuilinn path. Perhaps they represented too close a brush with the hoi-polloi: for the Journal records that the official party had signed the **second** page of the visitors' book that afternoon and expressed the hope that the first page which contained the names of surreptitious pre-opening visitors – 'members of the baser sort' in its own words – would soon be cut out by the Hut Custodian and 'consigned to the Allt a'Mhuilinn'!

Even after his days on the hill came to an end, he continued to serve the Club as their Guidebooks General Editor, until 1945 when advancing years (he was then 75) drove him to request 'retirement' from the post. They made him an Honorary Member in 1953, sixty years after his fresh-faced entry into their ranks.

His obituary in the SMC Journal in 1958 was naturally both full and effusive, written by the great mid-century climber J H B Bell.

> With the passing of the Rev. Archibald Aeneas Robertson, a great Scottish mountaineer and an honorary member of our Club, we may note the end of topographical exploration of the Bens and Glens of the Scottish Highlands...
> (SMCJ 26, p362)

An umbilical cord with the Club's great pioneers had finally been severed with his passing, this the SMC's Grand Old Man and the Munros' *an duine uasal*.

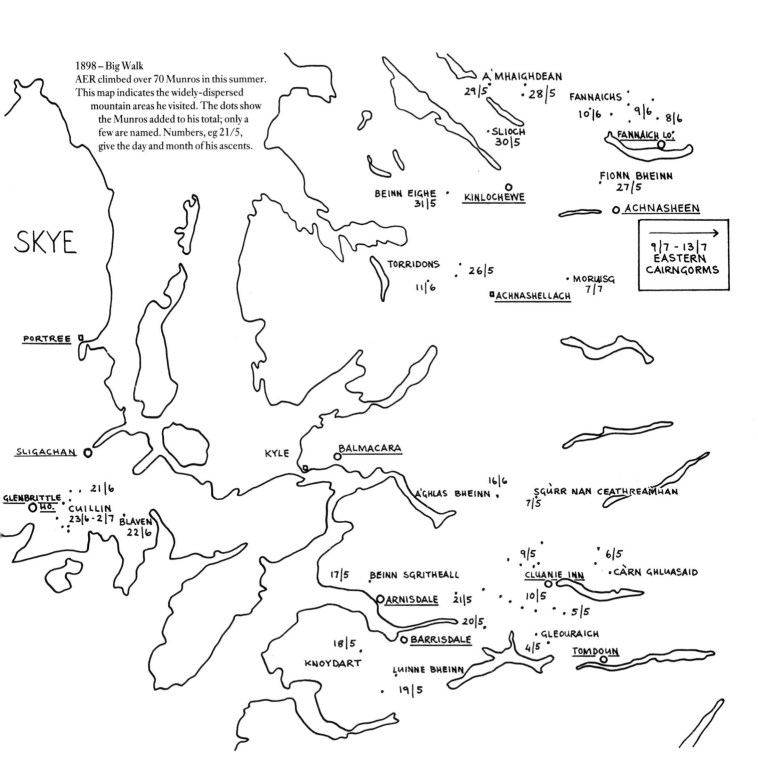

1898 – Big Walk
AER climbed over 70 Munros in this summer.
This map indicates the widely-dispersed
mountain areas he visited. The dots show
the Munros added to his total; only a
few are named. Numbers, eg 21/5,
give the day and month of his ascents.

SKYE

A'MHAIGHDEAN
29/5   • 28/5   FANNAICHS
                        10/6 •   • 9/6 • 8/6
        • SLIOCH
          30/5   FANNAICH LO.

                        FIONN BHEINN
BEINN EIGHE   • KINLOCHEWE   27/5
  31/5
                        • ACHNASHEEN

TORRIDONS   • MORUISG
        • 26/5   7/7
  11/6
        • ACHNASHELLACH

PORTREE   9/7 - 13/7
                                     EASTERN
                                     CAIRNGORMS

SLIGACHAN   KYLE   BALMACARA

GLENBRITTLE • • 21/6   A'GHLAS BHEINN •   16/6   SGÙRR NAN CEATHREAMHAN
  HO.   CUILLIN   7/5
      23/6-2/7 BLAVEN
                22/6   9/5   • 6/5
                                                                    • CÀRN GHLUASAID
                    17/5   BEINN SGRITHEALL   • CLUANIE INN
                                                     10/5
                          ○ ARNISDALE   21/5 • •
                                              • • 5/5
                          20/5
          18/5   ○ BARRISDALE   • GLEOURAICH
                                            4/5   TOMDOUN
          KNOYDART   LUINNE BHEINN

                    • 19/5

CHAPTER FOUR

The Big Walks

AER's greatest achievement when on course for his completion must surely be his two big walks in the early summers of 1898 and 1899, each three months long and each netting about seventy new Munros. Until Hamish Brown's 1977 Odyssey when all 277 Munros were climbed in a single four-month trip, Robertson's stamina on his two walks set a standard as much for the style in which his completion was done as for the final accomplishment.

There can be little doubt that he covered the ground on these big walks with his eyes clearly fixed on the prize of first and full completion of the Munros, since his itinerary picked out only those peaks new to him and avoided repetition. The very start of the first big walk in 1898 was, immediately upon alighting from the Edinburgh train, an afternoon ascent of Aonach Mor, after which he descended straight to Glen Spean so turning his back on Aonach Mor's close neighbour Aonach Beag (which he had already done). He cycled off north next day into unexplored country where he could bag new peaks. Again, in the middle of the 1899 trip, while collecting new summits in the Affric area, he proceeded from Beinn Fhionnlaidh to Mam Sodhail 'skirting Carn Eighe' which he had bagged before, but which lay in direct line.

The first big walk of 1898 hoovered up Munros around Cluanie and Knoydart, on Skye and in Letterewe, in Torridon and finally in the eastern Cairngorms. The 1899 walk cleaned up on the northern Highlands – starting with the most northerly, Ben Hope – the remainder of Torridon, the Affric and Cannich areas, the Treig and Dessary groups, Mull's solitary one, some residual Lorne peaks and finally hills in a broad arc around Dalwhinnie. This second trip was obviously far less tidy in pattern since, like all subsequent Munroists approaching the final run-in, there were awkward groups or singles left outstanding.

On both summers' holidays he climbed Munros on about half the days, and several other days were spent travelling between centres, sometimes by train but more often by bike. When we take into account time spent on family business – he took a week out of the 1898 trip for his mother's funeral, and the best part of two fortnights in 1899 to spend with his fiancée Kate – then his achievement seems the more intense.

As a reverend, the Sabbath was both spiritually and – usually – bodily a day of rest, and several of these days of recuperation and contemplation came after six hard days on the saddle or on the march. Only three of the

Cluanie Inn, Easter 1931.

twenty-one Sundays involved saw him on the move or on the hill. The first experience of climbing on the Sabbath could have seemed ominous, for he ascended A'Mhaighdean on Sunday 29th May 1898 in 'copious rain all day' and a superstitious man might have spotted divine retribution in the hand that delivered him a telegram two days later announcing his mother's death. It really is quite astonishing that he did venture out onto the hills on a Sunday at all, considering the widespread sabbatarian views then held throughout Scotland and especially in the north-west, and even more so that he was an ordained minister. Not a few local people must have been scandalised, and it shows just how strongly he must have felt about doing all the Munros. He did travel and climb on one Sunday the following year, but he obviously saw that as a 'work of necessity' in the course of completion, for he avoided Sunday ascents in subsequent years. Even on SMC Meets in the 20th century he spent Sundays 'loafing about' (to use his own words) while others took to the hill.

Much has been written in recent years about the difficulty of his achievement in an age before modern roads, cars and lightweight clothing. But that is to see the hills through auto-centric eyes, forgetting the burdens that modern Munro-baggers tend to impose upon themselves in making hill-days or weekends the tasty filling sandwiched between two very stale slices of long car trips from the cities. AER had the advantages of long holidays (available to him as a young assistant minister), and of friends with country house bases here and there such as Methven whose house near Balmacara was thrice a springboard for the tops in 1898. His bicycle, heavy though it was compared to modern lightweights, was unlikely to be mown down by

The Mallaig road W of Glenfinnan when there were no juggernauts.

a supermarket juggernaut in Glen Shiel or by a view-distracted tourist beside Loch Maree. And he had, relative to today, a light rucksack.

Light? A log entry of earlier years details what he took with him into the hills: the rucksack itself, a wettermantel (a heavy cape which he had had sent from its Munich manufacturer), a little food (he listed figs, raisins and chocolate), sometimes Uncle John's binoculars (scientific mountaineering again), a shirt and trousers, and ... his slippers! This last item gives the clue to this lightweight pack. For the glens were still inhabited and buildings that are now bothies were then still home to keepers and their families whose doors were open for bed and board to the few visitors who dropped in off the hill, especially a minister like himself.

So he needed neither sleeping bag nor stove, food nor fuel, as he traversed the hills. It is unlikely his pack reached even half the weight of Hamish Brown's pared-down 10kg pack. Of course his hobnailed boots would be heavier to lift and swing through the strides, but by comparison in the late 20th century, careful logistical planning and great expense on high-tech materials would be needed to support such extensive hill-wandering, and the spontaneity would be lost. AER also had, of course, the added impetus that comes from being an explorer in barely-charted territory, where the stone of the cairn-builder and the sole of the Munro-bagger had barely left their mentions on the mountains.

Of course his fare in these humble dwellings was naturally just what the people ate themselves, and it was probably a poverty-enforced vegetarianism eked out with fish. That is why, on his return to Shiel Bridge Inn after six days walking in Knoydart staying nights at such dwellings, to the serving girl's astonishment he 'gobbled up' the dish of cold roast, explaining that he had not eaten anything **meaty** (his emphasis) since leaving Balmacara nearly a week previously.

His bike was both a boon and a bane. A boon for the long approaches to the hills in the days before cars or buses, and a bane because he had to return to its hiding place in the heather. There was sometimes the nagging thought that it might not be there when he returned. Early in the 1898 walk, for instance, he left it to climb Creag a'Mhaim in the Cluanie range, but did so uneasily 'by reason of a party of tinkers whom I saw approaching.' In the rosy afterglow of completion he seems to have forgotten this, and dispensed this piece of advice to would-be disciples:

Don't be afraid your bike will run away or be stolen in your absence! Turn him loose in the heather, and he will be waiting for you when you return. (SMCJ 7, p11)

Sometimes he left his bike with trusty shepherds or at railway stations. Of course he had the great advantage, not available to modern travellers, that every train had a guard's van where bikes were accepted as a matter of course without pre-booking: the Sprinters have nothing on the old steam-hauled trains in that department! The bike was a means of portage as well as locomotion and on his 1899 walk he set off on a pannier-laden *Beesline Humber* with his ice-axe strapped along the top tube and Uncle John's binoculars sitting up in the front basket. He pedalled this pack-horse the 22 miles from Lairg to Altnaharra in just 3 hours, admittedly on a calm day with no head wind and with easy gradients. But this was no great feat for a man who had been a keen member of the CTC (Cyclists Touring Club) before taking to the hills (a common pattern in Scotland ever since), and his teenage diaries had logged regular trips of 30 miles, and summer totals of 600 miles.

The maps on pages 17 & 30 illustrate the ground he covered in the two summers' trips. There were highlights both on the tops and in the glens. On the tops the highlight of both years took place on offshore island Munros, in Skye in '98 and in Mull in '99.

The 1898 highlight took place on midsummer's day. Having already clocked up 45 Munros on the mainland that summer, he was spending a fortnight in the Cuillin in the company of that celebrated climbing couple the Inglis Clarks, and James Parker, all other than the distaff side being leading lights of the SMC. They rock-

The Pinnacle Ridge, Sgurr nan Gillean

climbed, scrambled and peak-bagged from their base at Sligachan Hotel. The very first day, June 21st, was surely AER's high point, for his account of their ascent of Pinnacle Ridge of Sgurr nan Gillean occupies three pages of his journal, the largest single day's entry in it. AER led up the fifth pinnacle.

> Half way up the usual route takes to the right up an easy gully. The rocks to the left were difficult and steep. I saw however that I could make them 'go' all right so I started up them … They were uncommon steep and you looked straight down 1000 feet, but the holds were magnificent and I shinned up them coming out at the summit just on the cairn. They were all delighted with my variation and voted it the best climbing of the day' (Log 1, p66)

We can see why he was proud of this special day on the hill. He continues in his journal, embellishing his

feat, by describing Sgurr nan Gillean as 'the most precipitous hill I have yet been on' and noting that a leap from the summit in any direction 'would easily relieve you of your life.'

This red letter day for him was capped by a view south when the clouds rolled away allowing WIC to take his famous photo entitled 'Blaven from Sgurr nan Gillean'. This appeared in the SMC Journal for September 1898 as illustration for an article by its taker entitled 'The mountaineer as a searcher after the beautiful', an essay in religiosity. He referred to this view of Blaven as an example of the contrast between peace and storm, and goes on to say that 'The enthusiastic mountaineer is tempted to exclaim – This is the very gate of heaven! – No doubt the good Reverend at his shutter elbow would have agreed with this sentiment.

Two days later they experienced little peace and real storm, having to turn back ten feet from the top of the Basteir Tooth as a screaming wind spreadeagled him on the rocks, and rain washed over them.

> Oh how cold I was! – I don't think I was ever so cold in all my life. Part of the way down was a gully which by this time was a torrent. I had to lie with the water pouring over me while I paid out the rope to Clark. When clear of the rocks we took to our heels and ran. *Ran*, gracious, we ran for miles, ending by coming up to the Inn at the double. I think the people thought we were mad. (Log 1, p68)

Then, confesses the Reverend to his journal, he had the largest amount of strong drink he had ever consumed in his life, half a tumbler of whisky dispensed by Clark, who had the same himself. Neat. The Reverend slept for an hour in his room, wakened to the dinner gong, lurched to the dining room, ate a hearty meal, and was in fine form next day. Clark however could not take his drink like a man of the cloth and was violently sick, spending the evening in bed. Through his befuddlement he might have been aware of the Reverend, and Parker, tut-tutting at the foot of his bed.

The drink might have had some delayed effect on our subject's brain, however. For his journal states 'no details recorded' of the ascents over the next few days of five other Munros on the ridge including Sgurr Dearg. This peak is overshadowed by the famous Inaccessible Pinnacle ('with an infinite drop on one side and an even longer drop on the other'), which was not at that time an official Munro, but whose ascent would surely have stuck out in memory as this blade of rock does on the hill. His friends left Skye at the end of June and he stayed on to bag his final Munro there, Sgurr na Banachdich, in the company of Dr Alfred Harker, a geologist working for the Geological Survey of Scotland, before crossing to the mainland to continue his quest. Over forty years later, AER wrote of this companion – who spent six years mapping the Cuillin – in an SMCJ obituary:

> ... we did Sgurr na Banachdich together. We went up to the Mam, into Coire na Creiche and round the base of Sgurr Thuilm. The rapidity with which Harker traversed the ground was quite remarkable, and the deft way he selected the easy and quick routes to gain his objectives, made a strong impression on me ...

1899's highlight was also on an island, also in June, with the ascent of Ben More in Mull. On the steamer, he went sailing to Salen on Mull in early afternoon, and cycled in an hour to the foot of the mountain. He stood on its top at 7 o'clock, and spent an hour there. This hour occupies a full page of his journal, the longest entry from then until completion day in 1901, and in it he waxes lyrical about the view:

> I have never seen the like of it either before or since – the sun setting into the Atlantic is making for itself, on the mist below, a shining path of light. As I sit watching and waiting and looking the wisps of mist are gathering together forming a thick ribbed cloud below me which is slowly creeping up the valley and rolling over the bealachs, leaving the tops bright and clear in the evening sun. Looking westward, the cloud has wholly covered Loch na Keal, leaving only the peak of Gometra rising, Proteus-like, out of the cloud sea. The shoulder of the hill below me is now shrouded, mantled in the wrinkled folds of white, and then, in the twinkling of an eye, the mantle is lifted off and it is all clear again. One could hardly tell where the mist ended and where the sea began. Along the line of the setting sun the rays have made a way for themselves and have pierced through the cloud mist, and you can see the sea along the path of light. (Log 2, p17)

Perhaps the mists of time were also shifting about in his memory (for the account was written several years later). For Gometra's island top at 500 feet is in fact hidden from Ben More's cairn by Ulva's two higher hills, and besides, just seven days before the summer

The Glenelg ferry with Kate and the tandem aboard

solstice, 8 o'clock is not a Hebridean sunset by several hours. That he wrote so much and so effusively is testimony enough to a moving mountain experience such as only the islands can provide so strongly.

Wave-girt islands were the stage for the two walks' highlights, and the western seas also murmur in the backcloth of some of his other adventures. In May 1898 he made a six-day trip to bag the Munros around Loch Hourn. He started it on board the steamer 'Claymore' while it fuelled at Kyle, sleeping on board until woken by the steward at 4 a.m. as it neared Glenelg, and was shipped ashore by the ferry. In the grey light of a rainy dawn he took shelter in a lowly cattle shed at Eileanreoch Farm. He was disturbed there *in flagrante* with his pipe by the farmer and his dogs at 6 a.m. The farmer, discovering he had not a dosser but a divine on his lands, invited him into the dining room and had the maids make him breakfast after he'd slept in the armchair until 9 a.m. As midday approached and the rain eased he finally tore himself from the tentacles of

cosy warmth and set off for the breezy slopes of Beinn Sgritheall, leaving behind, no doubt, some head-scratching at this curious traveller.

He inhaled the salt breezes again the next day, being ferried over Loch Hourn by an old crofter, retired from his days of sailing round the world. He was most impressed by the Reverend's alpenstock and observed 'Ah, that's a grand tomahawk that you've got,' to the great amusement of its owner. He went on to take the scalps of Ladhar Bheinn and the Knoydart Munros, returning over Sgurr na Sgine to the Shiel Inn (of meaty fame), and completed this six-day circle of the sea by taking the ferry from Totaig across Loch Duich, near its junction with Loch Alsh. There he had 'some fun in hooting with an old tin horn' to call the ferryman over.

Ferries thread the 1899 trip together too. Heading south from his northern start, he took the ferry across Loch Broom at Ullapool, and fortunately met a man on board who was well placed to help him push his loaded bike up a 'fearful steep hill', that being the 700 foot path climbing up and over to the Badrallach road that led him down to Dundonnell. Further on, he was boated across Loch Torridon to Shieldaig, and across Strome Ferry towards his Balmacara staging-post.

Adventures on the hill were comparatively rare, and even the weather rated a mention in his journals only in extremes. Incidents of any kind were minor. In 1898 he did manage to get briefly lost on the criss-crossing tracks north of Kinloch Hourn, and he fell into a peat bog on the descent to Shiel Inn: he felt obliged to wash his stockings and knickers (trousers) in a burn and to dry them on rocks before making his carnivorous entry through the inn's portals. On Sgorr Ruadh he did some scrambling with ropes, with a newly-met walker.

On Beinn Eighe he had to make a tricky descent in thick mist, and alone (after companion George Reid had turned back); a descent which, he wrote 'looked mighty bad' in retrospect and 'not a place for a man alone.'

The brief catalogue of relatively trivial incidents includes his first hill day in the 1899 trip, during what was to be a year of cold early summer, its effects magnified by his starting in the far north. During his ascent of Ben Klibreck that day his beard froze stiff and his landlady nearly did likewise with fear at the consequences of his venturing out on 'such an awful day', similar to one that had claimed a local shepherd a month previously. 'She did not know me!!', Robertson smiles to himself in his journal. And as late as May 20th that year he wrote:

> There is a lot of snow on the hills here yet. Every day I walk through acres of it. (Log 2, p10)

But we have to look hard for real adventure in his journal, and his ability to make drama out of trivia is perhaps highlighted by his finding space to recount, on the misty Beinn Eighe trip, that he had lost a stocking which he had been using as a muffler.

His two big walks were both in the spring and early summer when nature is on the move, released from winter's iron grip. But his eyes did not register much of that movement. No animals flit across the pages of his journal (unless we include the rats who disturbed his sleep at Inchrory), few birds, and there is but one splash of leaf green when he lunched in May 1899 in Glen Cannich '... in the most lovely birch wood you ever saw.' Perhaps. But his log immediately goes on to list in detail *not* the sylvan beauties but the contents of his lunch box!

His ornithology was very limited. Not surprisingly he was able to identify a golden eagle which he disturbed on top of Meall Buidhe in 1898, launching itself off over the corrie. And later that year he identified some broken ptarmigan's eggs just below the cairn of Carn Fhidhleir. The only other reference to birds on the two summers' walks came right at the end of the 1899 trip, on Carn Mairg:

> Saw a strange bird on C.M. Uttering a plaintive note, constantly repeated. Runs like a rat. Short straight black bill, longish legs. Greenish-brown mottled back, black belly and throat, a little white on breast and sides. Black legs – not red – black eyes. Short tail. (Log 2, p21)

Not one for twitchers, this, since it is probably the (very common) golden plover. Our man in the mountains was certainly no Seton-Gordon!

If the colour of nature and the drama of adventure were not the stuff of his two big walks, what does come across more three-dimensionally is his record of contacts with the people. He mixed and stayed with all classes, from cottars to keepers to captains and capitalists.

In 1898 he hobnobbed with the Duke of Abercorn ('his Grace', indeed) at Achnasheen Hotel, who asked him 'all kinds of questions about the hills' and who was 'very kind and affable'. And at the other end of the social scale he had to throw his stockings at the noisy swarm of rats which attacked his sandwiches in the bothy at Inchrory! On the 1898 walk he stayed with keepers (at Barrisdale, Fannich and Inchrory) or simply had tea with them. Thus there was a 'splendid tea with the keeper's wife (or sister?)' [his question] at Lianachan and a similar spread at Alltbeithe (now the Glen Affric Youth Hostel). He describes his hostess:

> Mrs Scott was a fine young Shetland woman and was very busy sorting and carding wool that afternoon. (Log 1, p51)

McMaster the keeper at Barrisdale had holidaying friends staying who shot rats and played the bagpipes for amusement – forefathers of the Creag Dhu club, perhaps? With two keepers he actually climbed mountains, at Slioch and in the Fannichs. In the latter case Fraser the keeper rowed him over the loch and climbed with him on two days. On the third day he rowed him to the west end but declined to climb, and the rather ungrateful Robertson says that '... He had had enough of climbing the last two days, being fat and lazy.'

Sometimes his welcome was open-armed and generous (as at Eileanreoch Farm), sometimes sumptuous (at Kyleakin after the 1898 Cuillin climbing trip he 'was taken in hand by an Indian servant and bathed and dressed like a baby in luxurious comfort'), sometimes plain and wholesome as at the famous Maggie Gruer's at Inverey near Braemar. This remarkable woman's cottage door was to admit many of the famous names of Scottish climbing and walking, like J H B Bell and Janet Adam Smith, as well as hundreds of ordinary walkers seeking a night's shelter, and she treated them all alike as befitted a good egalitarian. (She was a Liberal, and later a Labour, supporter.) She fought prominently for the rights of the local people, tenants or not, to take in visitors – and the grouse-moor set ('chappies wha' set up the boardies wi' them screedies') were the butt of her sardonic humour. What she made of AER is not known, but he would have been made welcome for no-one was ever turned away from her house, even when it got busier after the first war, with sleepers occupying every corner, and all being fed their statutory eggs. His journal certainly notes that '... I found comfortable quarters for several days at Miss Gruer's.' He would have been one of her earlier guests, presaging the 20th century mass movement into the hills, for she was aged but 36 when he stayed, in a life which spanned nearly eight decades with Gaelic at its anchor point and English at its fraying end. The fact however that he had no tales to tell of her, unlike those told by other travellers like J H B Bell[1] and Janet Adam Smith,[2] suggests that the 'common touch' did not come too easily to him in dealing with ordinary people.

Although he mixed with all social classes on these walks, there were always members of his own class

Black House, Morar.

nearby to whom he could retreat. For instance he gave Skiary on Loch Hourn a miss on discovering that it was not only 'damp, dark and dirty' but also dry–'there was neither beer nor whisky in the place'–and he moved on to seek shelter at the nearby house of Captain Campbell, captain of Lord Burton's yacht (don't you know!). Sir Hugh Munro *did* stay at Skiary in 1899, after fishing for codlings on Loch Hourn. He described it thus:

> Skiary must certainly be one of the most primitive inns(!) in Europe. A beehive crofter's cottage on the shores of the loch, with just a 'but and a ben', and, but for the codlings, I should have been dependent on oatmeal and very bad whisky, which probably had contributed nothing to the revenue of the United Kingdom. (SMCJ 15, p68)

AER spent several spells on the 1898 trip at Methven's, a friend with a substantial house at

Benula Lodge where AER would have found hospitality: now under the combined waters of Loch Mullardoch and Loch Lungard.

Coillemor near Balmacara, and he ended the walk staying with the Dowie Urquharts at their Ballater summer house, back in the embraces of the well-to-do.

1899's walk had a similar socially-mixed pattern, but was varied by more sojourns at hotels such as Altnaharra where he dined on freshly-caught salmon, and had the left-overs with the breakfast egg and bacon; and at the houses of the middle classes, as well as keepers. He stayed at more places too, often going to an area without a prior recommendation, this suggesting that he had gained in social confidence from the previous walk in the taking of social risks that such dropping-in entailed. Some of them were, as he himself wryly noted, downright unenthusiastic at his stay (such as the MacLarens of Glen Affric).

Others he got on with like a house on fire, such as young Finlayson the keeper at the west end of Loch Mullardoch who agreed immediately to put up this total stranger with the proviso '… that we are not prepared for a gentleman like you.' Robertson took to this display of deference and he describes this 'decent fellow' in these words:

> He is quite a young fellow – say 24 – ⟨AER himself was all of 29 then!⟩ but one of the best of his kind I've ever met. So intelligent, so eager for knowledge. He is not married but has a fine old housekeeper (Flora) who does things very well. She has not 'the English' or at least very little of it and you would laugh to hear her and me at it. He has got a fine wee house (Coire nan Cuilean) all beautifully lined with wood inside and 'as dry as a cork' to use his own expression. He came here from Camban. He is a great reader and the books he has

Mrs McDonnel, Ardchuik, Glen Strathfarrar

astonish me. Travel books of all sorts, about fifty of them. We have great cracks and the interest he takes in my maps, aneroid compass and my knowledge of the district is quite touching. (Log 2, p11)

He stayed with Finlayson for four days, and together they climbed Beinn Fionnlaidh on a ten-hour day that stretched over Mam Sodhail and An Socach. But this was hardly a relationship of equals, more that of a teacher and an amenable lad o' pairts. It's significant that their friendship (an easy one for AER to handle as the dominant figure) provides the longest character sketch in his journals. Even the keeper he had stayed with just before this, McDonnel of Ardchuik (sic), who treated him to dinners (not mere teas) in the evenings and who climbed Sgurr Fhuar-thuill with him did not get as much coverage. And others like the Torridon keeper McDonald who climbed Beinn Alligin and

Liathach with him, Ross at Loch Treig who put him up in his lightning-struck cottage, and old acquaintance McIntosh at Luiblea, got but passing mention.

It would be unfair to accuse Robertson of being happiest in the master-servant set-up that seems to underlie his affection for Finlayson, for that would be to judge him by modern social standards by which he would assuredly be found guilty. In late Victorian times it would have been very difficult if not impossible to have developed equal relationships in such a heavily banded society. And it is not surprising to find a faintly patronising picture of the Highland people, almost a picture of 'noble savages' in the Victorian idiom, emerging from his 1901 article *The 'Munro's' of Scotland* (sic) which is worth quoting at length as much for what it tells us about its author as about its subjects:

Towards evening you approach the keeper's house not without apprehension, the dogs rush out barking vociferously, half in welcome, half in anger. You knock at the door, there is a parley. You are admitted, and once admitted, treated with all the courtesy, dignity and hospitality that are the prime characteristics of the Celtic nature. In all my wanderings I have never been refused a night's shelter. The Highlander is nothing if not hospitable. Of course this has to be gone about in the right way. If a man comes up to a keeper's house and demands a bed in the same tone of voice as he would engage a room at the Metropole he will be refused – and quite right too – for even a Highlander's house is his castle. But if he approaches his would-be host and hostess with fitting politeness with a certain sense of obligation

28

McPhail, East Monar

Ben Alder Cottage with Mrs McCook.

in his voice and bearing, he will certainly be received and welcomed ... What lonely lives they lead, an isolation scarcely credible in these days ... And what naive ideas many of them have! I well remember the air with which one good woman opened the door of a tiny room in which was a sitz-bath standing up on end, and the pride with which she exclaimed, 'This is the bath-room, if such a thing should ever be required.'

... And what pawky humour too ... let one reminiscence suffice.

'Well Donald', I remarked one evening as we sat with our pipes over the peat fire, 'this must be a wild place in winter.' 'Oh yes, sir, a wild place in the winter time.' 'Big storms, I daresay.' 'Hoo yes, storms ... and wrecks' 'And strange animals perhaps?' 'Heuch aye ... and sea serpents, great sea serpents. There was waane, it wass two years ago, her heid cam thro' the Kyle on the 7th of June, and

it wass the 12th of August before her tail passed oot. I wass tired waatching her.' (SMCJ 7, p12)

The picture that emerges of Robertson from this article suggests an avuncular figure, definitely part of the family, proud of the junior members, and just a bit prone to head-patting.

With one particular keeper and his family he formed what became a life-long friendship. He first met the McCooks of Ben Alder cottage in 1893, while on a solo cross-country trip. As with Finlayson, the basis of the friendship seems to have been laid in the initial deferential reply:

I had heard from the keeper at Aviemore of possible night quarters at Ben Alder Lodge (McCook's), so I descended (Ben Alder) by the south-east shoulder and reached McCook's at 5.35. With some trepidation I knocked at the door.

Out comes Mrs McCook, smiling and neat and clean as she always is. 'Can you put me up for the night?' 'Yes, sir, we shall be delighted.' Thus was I admitted to McCook's, and in the many times I have revisited I have always gone with the greatest pleasure and been received with the greatest courtesy.' (Log 1, p14)

Among the 'many times' was an interlude in his 1899 trip when he and his fiancée Kate stayed there for a fortnight. Modesty, perhaps, bade him give scant details of their activities on that holiday, though they did climb Ben Alder by the Long Leachas ridge and also the Corrour Munros: his personal diary notes that he paid the McCooks £2.50 for their stay, a fair sum at that time, a third of his monthly stipend. In later years he was able to repay Mr McCook in a different way by discounting, in print, the rumours that he had eventually committed suicide in Ben Alder cottage thus causing it to be haunted.

Other places where he found accommodation in 1899 have a familiar ring even today, with the Clachaig Inn and the Kingshouse in Glencoe, the Stage House Inn at Glenfinnan, the Inveroran and Dundonnell

Hotels all featuring. Others were more novel. His quarters included Inverlael Farm in the north-west, a forester's house at Invergarry, a schoolhouse at Loch Etive ('where the schoolteacher made me most comfortable for two nights'), the Reverend McLennan of Laggan Free Church (surely an early instance of ecumenicism), and the station master's house at Dalwhinnie (perhaps here, right at the end of his walk, he was running short of cash for hotels!) What a contrast to today's long-distance walkers who have to mix either in politely anodyne B&Bs, or in bothies or campsites only with fellow-walkers: the reverend got a cross-section of Highland society as varied from top to bottom as his vertical movement up and down the land's contours. And he finished this the second of his big walks in style. Cycling from the station master's at Dalwhinnie to Drumochter, he left his bike in the heather and *ran* to the top of Sgairneach Mhor, then remounted and rode all the way to Perth – 'a quick day' he wrote. A short trip to end a long walk!

1. *A Progress in Mountaineering:* J H B Bell (Oliver & Boyd, 1950) Reprinted as *Bell's Scottish Climbs* (Gollanz, 1990)
2. *Mountain Holidays:* Janet Adam Smith (Dent, 1946)

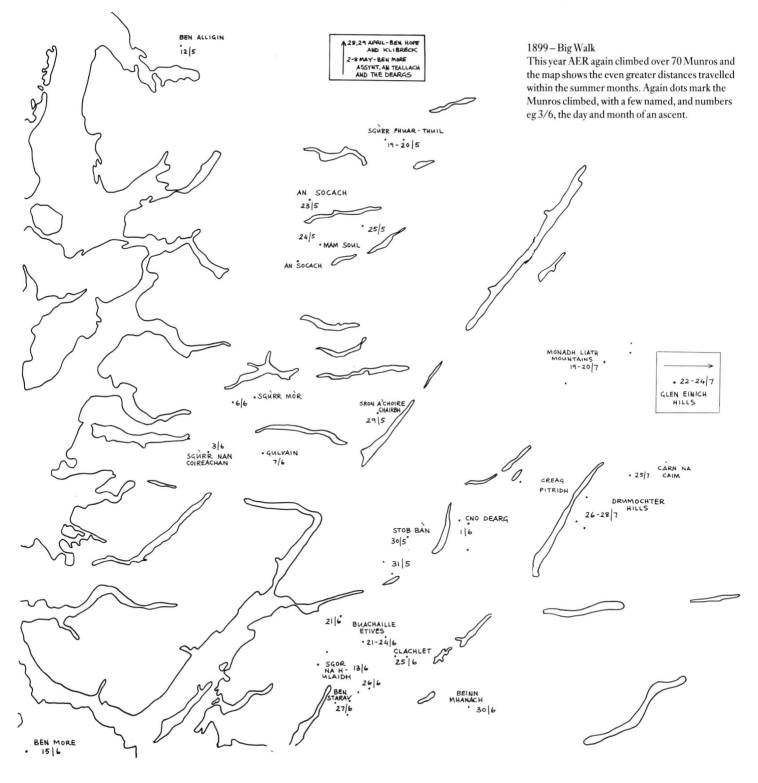

BEN ALLIGIN
12/5

28,29 APRIL - BEN HOPE
AND KLIBRECK
2-8 MAY - BEN MORE
ASSYNT, AN TEALLACH
AND THE DEARGS

1899 – Big Walk
This year AER again climbed over 70 Munros and
the map shows the even greater distances travelled
within the summer months. Again dots mark the
Munros climbed, with a few named, and numbers
eg 3/6, the day and month of an ascent.

SGÙRR FHUAR - THUIL
19 - 20/5

AN SOCACH
23/5

24/5   25/5
· MAM SOUL

AN SOCACH

MONADH LIATH
MOUNTAINS
19 - 20/7

22 - 24/7
GLEN EINICH
HILLS

· 6/6   · SGÙRR MÒR

SRON A'CHOIRE
GHAIRBH
29/5

CÀRN NA
CAIM
· 25/7

CREAG
PITRIDH

3/6
SGÙRR NAN
COIREACHAN   · GULVAIN
7/6

DRUMOCHTER
HILLS
26 - 28/7

· CNO DEARG
STOB BÀN   1/6
30/5

31/5

21/6   BUACHAILLE
ETIVES
· 21 - 24/6

CLACHLET
25/6

· SGOR   13/6
NA H-
ULAIDH
26/6

BEN
STARAV   BEINN
27/6   MHANACH
· 30/6

BEN MORE
15/6

CHAPTER FIVE

The Life and Times of a Gentleman

When AER died in 1958 his obituary in the SMC Journal said that his death marked the end of an era, the era of topographical exploration of the Scottish mountains. It might also have said that it was the end of the era in which the moneyed social classes dominated Scottish mountaineering. Many sports have followed this pattern, particularly those requiring equipment like golf or sailing, being taken up first by those who could afford it. Mountaineering has been, especially since the Second World War, the recreation of everyman as the tide of affluence has spread down society to float all but the poorest off the bedrock of poverty: but of necessity in late Victorian times it was initially the preserve of the well-to-do. AER's birth, his marriages and his death, all took place against an affluent backdrop, and it was this relative wealth which enabled not only his private education but also his pursual of his hill-walking and other hobbies. Mammon was as important as Munros in his life, though it must be said that he actively pursued only the latter while, happily for him, being in passive receipt of the former.

He was born in 1870, the only son of a Victorian merchant residing among the salubrious villas of Helensburgh. Subsequent addresses include Bridge of Allan, and then in Edinburgh initially at Whitehouse Loan and ultimately at Cluny Gardens, all affluent addresses then as now. Without the discreet chink of this wealth he would never have had his private schooling at Glasgow Academy nor his MA and BD

courses at Glasgow and Edinburgh Universities, in the days before student grants and loans. Without it he would never have had the opportunity to go, as he did, on a two-month American holiday in 1891, nor on his European tour through Paris to Italy and Vesuvius in 1898, the tour which seemed to spark his determination to complete the Munros. Nor could he ever have got beyond a distant glimpse of the mountains on the blue skyline, since the purchase of mountaineering equipment, of travel, of hotel accommodation and of the time to spend weeks or months in the hills were far beyond the reach of most of the population in late Victorian times.

The purchase of a camera and all the necessary developing equipment was still the preserve of the Edwardian well-to-do in the early 20th century. Without his wealth too he could hardly have afforded to retire from the ministry at the age of 49, to spend a long and comfortable 'retirement' in the very substantial stone-built semi-detached house at Cluny Gardens (now flatted into two still-substantial homes). This enabled him to devote so much time to hobbies like woodworking, to new interests such as his motor-car, to being the SMC's Grand Old Man figure in the early thirties, to being a figurehead in the Scottish Right of Way Society and the Royal Scottish Geographical Society and various other quangos. His release from day-to-day burdens was sufficient to allow him to do 'good works' such as being Chaplain to the nearby Astley Ainslie hospital for 15 years. None of these things could have been financed from his ministerial stipend (at £8-6s-8d a month in the late 1890s, for instance) and his private means certainly came from his parents (he could afford, in 1895, to put his ailing mother into private care at Craig House in Edinburgh), from his aunts from whom he also inherited, and also from judicious marriages within the 'right circles'.

Socially his circle was as restricted in society as much as his means were liberating, and it was confined to the better-off. At play the then Scottish Mountaineering Club spanned all social classes from landowners to lawyers, doctors to divines, merchants to ministers, and professors to publishers ... but little else. This was naturally a circumstance born of necessity in the social and economic state of the times. (We discuss in chapter 2 how he was drawn to the hills as much by the social company as by the sport itself.) The SMC Journal's description of the Easter 1903 Skye Meet illustrates the atmosphere in the Sligachan Hotel in the evenings:

> Possibly owing to the weather, there was abundance of animated conversation. As usual the Church claimed complete freedom of speech in its native wilds. A brisk commission business was done in gloves and wettermantels. The great question of colloids and crystoids was brought one step nearer solution, and we had an eloquent statement of what may be termed the Munro Doctrine, viz, the strict, almost fanatical recognition of the exclusive rights of private property in land. (SMCJ 7, p282)

At work the role of minister was a more pedestalled one than in the modern populist age. So while he was a young assistant minister at Musselburgh's North Esk church and then at Edinburgh Morningside (pronounced Moaningsade by many of its denizens!) at St Matthew's church, he was dined (if not wined) almost every evening by some or other middle-class

family from the congregation, anxious for a socially suitable guest to grace their table. When minister at Braes of Rannoch parish, he mixed with the local gentry (who certainly would have had a hand in his selection for the job), and in particular Lord and Lady Menzies get several honourable mentions in his diaries. (In those days the minister was essentially paid by the teinds, the predecessor of the rates, and levied only upon the wealthy, like the local landowners.) He numbered Law Lords among his friends and acquaintances. His old climbing partner Sandy Moncrieff became Lord Moncrieff, Lord Justice Clerk in 1947: and one of the obituaries AER wrote in the SMC Journal was for Lord MacMillan, an Appeal Judge and apparently an expert at upper-crust drum-ups, being a dab hand at 'juniper fires, and outdoor meals'!

It is no surprise to find that he was politically a Conservative: his application to join the party was accepted in 1906, shortly before he got the charge of Rannoch parish. During the General Strike of 1926 he enrolled as a Special Constable, doing his bit, as he doubtless saw it, to stem the looming red whirlwind from stripping leafy Morningside. His diary records that things were 'pretty lively' at his allocated duty point at the city's Leith Docks and that the dockers 'were menacing' in manner. Mind you, a gentleman of leisure down from Morningside to police the strike can hardly have expected the meek to inherit the picket lines!

His two marriages were made from these same affluent social circles; his second wife was a relative of the millionaire Lord Burrell, who gifted his collection to Glasgow. His first wife, Katherine Clusan McFarlan, appears to have been a relative. In a note in one of his hill-walking journals he refers to her as his cousin, and

AER's first wife, Kate.

Climbed Meall Dearg with A. and Sandy. A. has now climbed all the 3000 foot hills in Scotland. Drank his health at the top and after we came down. Grand day!

Hardly a eulogy, but perhaps she was a mite miffed because he had, on top 'kissed the cairn and then his wife' in that order! In 1904 she accompanied him on a trip to the Cuillin, and in the care of the celebrated guide, John MacKenzie, (after whom the peak Sgurr Mhic Choinnich was named) whom AER had 'booked' for the week, she managed the traverse of the Basteir Tooth pinnacle. How undignified then that on the following day she sprained her ankle not on a rock slope but in falling off the pony on which she was being led up a mountain path. Her superior age meant that her health began to decline before his, and she died in the mid-1930s after a long illness. She was replaced with eyebrow-raising rapidity by a relatively young thing

certainly she came from Greenock, his mother's home town. Judging from her diaries which begin in 1872 (when AER would still have been in nappies) she must have been at least fifteen years his senior, so that when he married her in 1900 after a six-year courtship he would have been 30, she 45 or so, rather an unusual age-pairing! The family seemed to approve of the arrangement, for his diaries sometimes record his return from a day on the hill 'to meet Mother and Kate' who had spent the day more decorously. Their honeymoon must have been quite an expensive affair, involving hotels and travel from Dumfries to Aberdeen via Biggar, Blair Atholl, Pitlochry and Dalnaspidal.

He may have been considerably her junior but she seems to have been fit enough to share hill-days with him. They spent, for instance, a fortnight together exploring from Ben Alder cottage in 1889 on a 'pre-honeymoon'. And she accompanied him to the summit of his final Munro in 1901, as her own diary records:

AER's second wife, Winifred, Cluanie burn, June 1935.

(20 years his junior), Winifred Hutchison of Glasgow, with whom he had corresponded even before his first wife's death. She told an old friend of their first meeting. She had admired some photographs on display, and he had beamed, "I'm so glad you like them, Miss Hutchison, because *I* took them." – a more seemly line than the apocryphal invitation to view one's etchings.

She was of course more able to accompany him on the hill for the few more years he could manage, as well as to put a new spring in his step. A newspaper item of the late 1930s, eulogising this born-again couple as 'Mr and Mrs Mountaineer', relates:

> Mr Archibald Robertson has climbed every Munro. And now Mrs Robertson is doing her best to catch up with her husband. Last week she came back from Clova and ticked three more 3000 footers off HER list. This brought her total to 210 ...
> Mr and Mrs Robertson say there's nothing like climbing mountains together. It's the perfect pastime for a man and wife ...
> Now Mr Robertson has almost retired from active mountaineering ... Mrs Robertson who is younger keeps going. She'll be in the Cairngorms again at the end of this month, tackling more mountains on her husband's list.

Their relationship on the hills was not one of equals, or so it appears from a story of one day when they were climbing on snow, and he wished her to take a picture of him against a certain background. She made to cross over to the spot indicated, but he reproved her for making footsteps that would appear in the frame, and insisted that she descend some considerable distance and then go up again, to avoid this. She complied, without demur! She was however an accomplished hill-person in her own right, with a particular interest in mountain flora, and was a leading member of the Ladies Scottish Climbing Club. She wrote articles and poems for their journal, and was a leading force in their campaign to acquire a club hut at Black Rock, Rannoch Moor, just after the war. She and AER weathered an equinoctial gale there overnight in 1949, when he was seventy-nine, just a year after she and three friends spent a few days there in 'a sort of little oasis when ... one feels about sixteen again.'

Their last Munro together was Clachlet in 1940 (when AER was 70 years old), but she cannot have completed the Munros herself for she is not listed in the SMC's Roll of *Compleaters*. Being two decades younger than him, she not unnaturally survived his death in 1958, and for twenty years was a formidable little old Morningside lady, by repute the terror of tradesmen, but still a friend of the hills and hill-goers. She wrote on botanical matters for the LSCC Journal, and led nature rambles of the Lothians Nature Society. Until well into her seventies, she walked with a friend over the Pentlands, where her photographic memory of places was invaluable for navigation in mist. Shortly before her death she was introduced to Hamish Brown whose completion of all the Munros in one trip in 1977 had echoed her husband's achievement of seven decades earlier, when she was still a young girl. There were no children from either of AER's marriages (not surprisingly in view of the late-forties age of both his brides) and Winifred's death in 1978 cul-de-sacked that particular branch of the Robertson clan.

The wealth that had fuelled his mountaineering, and

had put the central heating in his marriages, also oiled the hinges of the manse door to his career, as well as providing the lubrication for his many interests and hobbies.

The profession of minister was often one which wealthy families put a son to so as to ensure a halo of respectability over the family name. A university degree followed by the theological licentiate was as accessible to the poor as the eye of the proverbial needle, but not to the scions of the wealthy. Not that there was any question of young Archibald's intelligence, for at school he gained first class certificates in subjects like Steam (Elementary Stages), Solid Geometry and Practical Plane, and Machine Construction. His reading while at University included Horace in the original, and he seems to have done well enough in Lord Kelvin's class in Natural Philosophy (physics) to have received special help from him in later years in obtaining an aneroid barometer.

His ministerial career seems to have struggled to get airborne for although he served as assistant minister in two Lothian parishes, the latter (St Matthews) being very socially desirable, it took him well over a decade until the age of 36 to obtain a parish of his own, Braes of Rannoch in Perthshire. In the old phrase he was becoming what is known as 'a stickit meenister', unable to move into a pulpit of his own. Perhaps he smoothed the path to it by learning Gaelic, for even today, 90 years later, that parish is a 'Gaelic-preference' parish with theoretical priority for a Gaelic speaker as minister. AER was clearly not a native Gaelic speaker (as many of the Rannoch parishioners would have been then), for an Anglicised Scots would have been his 'natural speak', and his misspellings of Gaelic hill-names in his journals

(such as Lurven for Ladhar Bheinn) would have caused a lot of rotating in cemeteries in the Gaidhealtachd. In 1904, perhaps with an eye to career opportunities, he embarked on a series of Gaelic lessons, with two series of thirty classes that spring and autumn. Since they were given on a one-to-one basis in his own home by native speakers (Mr McLeod and Mr McNab), at the rate of three a week, his wealth must have been useful again, this time for the loosening of tongues! A working knowledge of Gaelic would have been a useful part of his curriculum vitae when applying for the Rannoch parish a year or so later. Many years later he felt sufficiently familiar with the language to write a review for the SMC Journal in which he comments favourably, if slightly patronisingly, on the seminal work on Scottish Gaelic place-names by Professor of Celtic, W J Watson.

Being a minister in this small country parish was hardly arduous, and his diary reflects little business other than the obligatory services and the occasional

Braes of Rannoch manse, April 1908.

funeral. The manse of the Braes of Rannoch church, now a private holiday home after a spell as a Forestry Commission workers' hostel, stands on a knoll beside the bridge over the deep pools of the River Gaur, upstream of Loch Rannoch. The only material record of his sojourn there is a dog's gravestone in the garden inscribed 'Cato – faithful servant. 1909-1913'. But it was here that – in addition to passing fads like fishing the pools – two of his other great interests in life were pursued, photography and woodwork, to the virtual exclusion of the mountains on his literal doorstep. Ministers were reasonably well paid at that time, and together with the presence of servants doing most of the housework, he would have had plenty of time and the means to follow such inclinations.

The photographic bug had first bitten him in 1903, after he had completed the Munros. But the incubation period began earlier for his interest would have been aroused by various lantern slide lectures at the Club, and by the excellent work of members such as Lamond Howie, and William Inglis Clark with whom he frequently socialised. He saw the latter for advice about the purchase of a camera for the hills in late 1902, bought one in early 1903, and – his diary exclaims – 'Took my first photo!' in March that year. He had been experimenting with the developing and printing of other people's photos a few months previously. He had become the SMC's Slide Custodian, and could see the need to fill a gap in the collection caused by the absence of pictures of the north-west. He went out himself to fill that gap in June 1903 on a tour through the hills, many of which appeared in the first edition of the Club's Guide to that area. His breakthrough to the hallowed photo gallery of the Journal's pages came as early as

AER at work near Achallader, March 1925.

September 1903 when a picture of the snow-streaked Cuillin ridge taken at the Easter 1903 Meet appeared over his name, but it was 1905 before several of his pictures were featuring regularly.

Being an enthusiastic photographer was no mean task in those days. Carrying a whole plate camera, with wooden tripod legs and the necessary glass plates, would have involved lugging an awkwardly-shaped, 5-10 kg weight up hill and down glen. And there were no instant 'snaps': once a photographic opportunity arose, a minute or two would have to be spent setting up the tripod, getting its legs adjusted for the slope of the ground, composing the subject, and operating the shutter from under the black cloth, regardless of wind and weather. And pity the poor subjects, if they were human, having to stand posed or poised, perhaps in a dramatic position, while the muffled shouts from under the cloth urged them to move or whatever – no mere four seconds freeze-and-cheese for them! Perhaps this is why the climbers in many of these early photographs either look rather posed (as in the famous one showing four climbers ascending the snow slopes of Ben Lui's central gully) or are absent altogether, in contrast to today's obligatory cagouled back at the corner of the picture.

And the hill-work with the camera was only a beginning, for the return home signalled the start of many hours of developing and printing, labours which were to occupy much time in the Rannoch manse. Not as many however, as his new-found passion for woodworking. It seems to have started out as a work of necessity, making roofs and floors for a manse outhouse, but he was soon engaged in making panels for the communion table for the little church across the river, which can still be seen. His interest was sufficiently up and running by 1910 for him to make himself an inscribed tool-chest. And as with so many of his interests in life it soon came to be an all-consuming passion. By 1916, for instance, his diaries record little else but that of a man spending his days woodworking and furniture-making and polishing, with every humdrum detail noted. Even the hills outside seem to have disappeared in a cloud of sawdust, and his ankles to have been chained by wood-shavings, for this is the part of his life when he lived beside the hills physically but seemed to have little mental interest in them. The critical twice-yearly weekends of SMC Meets, at New Year and Easter, passed at Rannoch with dovetails being made, shelves being polished. O templates, O Munros!

When he moved to his Edinburgh house in 1920 the passion continued unabated. One room in the Cluny Gardens house was turned over to it – later buyers of the property had to have it rid of the woodworm that had come to infest that room – and a visitor can still see

Mahogany fireplace built by AER at the Cluny Gardens house. Photo by P Drummond.

there the results of his craftsmanship. After entering by the heavy oak door made by him, and proceeding along a hall floored with oaken parquet, a turn into the lounge reveals the superb mahogany fireplace lovingly-crafted by him. There is a story that, when his first wife was terminally ill, a friend discovered him in the woodwork room in the house assembling a coffin! Reproved by the friend, he desisted, but some of the distinctively-shaped panels were later incorporated into interior door panels. The story may of course be apocryphal...

As a gesture to his old passion of hill-walking, he made the table for the CIC Hut on Ben Nevis at which he performed the opening blessing, and which is still there after over sixty years of hard use, an enduring testimony to his skill. But even after age had shackled his hill-legs he was still found bent over the woodworking bench: as late as 1947 (at the age of 77) he was engaged in correspondence with the factor of

Colonsay for the purchase of a half-share in a fine old mahogany log. He intended to use it to make a vessel for holding Iona Abbey's communion linen, and also two trays for the island's landlord Lord Strathcona – for Lords as well as The Lord still figured highly in his elite social world.

Living to the age of 88 is not unusual nowadays with the availability of the National Health Service and the general improvement in living standards. But for a man born in 1870 it was unusual. AER was not a particularly healthy individual, his diaries recording frequent spells in bed after 'being colded'. He must have had a reasonably strong constitution to climb the hills and carry the plate camera; but being well-housed in substantial dwellings, having the services of servants (in a 1953 letter he bemoans the couple's fate after the loss of their maid at Cluny Gardens), and having the money to live well and to engage in healthy outdoor pursuits, all these stretched out his mortal span from Queen to Queen, from Victoria to Elizabeth. The life and times of a gentleman were not only full but also long.

Part Two: Background

CHAPTER SIX

Mountaineering Pioneers

The Reverend Robertson's achievement in completing
the ascent of all the known peaks over 3000 ft in
Scotland in 1901 was very much a maverick exploit. His
completion remained unrepeated for 22 years – by
another man of the cloth, the Reverend Burn. Although
there was a Salvationist contingent in the club which
eschewed difficulty and limited itself to hill-walking,
no-one else in the early SMC, apart from Munro
himself, appears to have been aiming at completion.

It is interesting to note that, though Munro and
Robertson were similar in interests and abilities with
respect to mountaineering, and both active Tories, they
did not appear to have enjoyed each others' company, or
to have teamed up on Meets. Perhaps Robertson's
attitude toward access upset Munro, who did many of
his ascents at night to minimise inconvenience to the
landed proprietors!

The priority of most of the early members of the
SMC was climbing – both summer rock-climbing and
snow and ice winter climbing. The period in which
Robertson took up mountaineering saw the summer
ascent of North-East Buttress and the winter ascent of
Tower Ridge on Ben Nevis by, respectively, the
Hopkinson brothers in 1892, and Collie, Solly and
Collier in 1894. Then in 1895 Tough and Brown did
the eponymous Ridge on Lochnagar and the following

North-East Buttress and Tower Ridge.

year Naismith ascended Crowberry Ridge on the
Buachaille. Harold Raeburn joined the club in 1896
and for the next twenty years could probably be said to
be the foremost Scottish climber, with the Church Door
Buttress on Bidean, Raeburn's Gully on Lochnagar and
a solo ascent of Observatory Ridge on Ben Nevis being
amongst his early first ascents. His conquest of
Raeburn's Arête on the Ben in 1902 with Dr. and Mrs.
Inglis Clark was one of the hardest rock climbs in
Scotland at that date and, of course, his phenomenal
winter ascent of Green Gully on the Ben in 1907 was
decades ahead of its time.

This then, briefly, was the context of activity in which
Robertson joined the club and took up mountaineering.
However, it should be pointed out that his own climbing

credentials were less impressive than those of many of his peers – indeed it is questionable whether the first Munroist and one-time Club President would today be admitted as a SMC member. Admission standards were lower in those days, and when AER joined in 1893 it was on the basis of an impressive tally of Munros already completed. In his sympathetic obituary of Robertson, J H B Bell wrote,

> It would be wrong to consider that his climbing was restricted to expeditions devoid of technical difficulty ... AER did some good rock climbs in his day. (SMCJ 26, p362.)

Robertson's own contribution to the SMC Journal, and his private Log-Book tend rather to show that he was a competent scrambler, and able to cope with rock-climbing of up to Very Difficult standard – though not leading – and with winter expenditions of up to Grade II in severity. Much – though not all – of his use of four rather than two limbs on the mountains was concentrated on the period between finishing his Munros in 1901 and his being ordained as minister at Braes of Rannoch in 1907.

Robertson acquired an ice-axe in the spring of 1893 and set off, 'immensely proud', to climb Cruachan on April 1st. He achieved the summit of Stob Garbh, 'not bad for a first snow climb', but observed that on the way down,

> ...we all slid away with howls of delight, nearly killing ourselves several times...how some of us did not do so is a mystery to me. (Log p9)

The next day saw more adventure on Ben Lui, and a 'pretty sharp lesson on how to respect a cornice';

> I gained the ridge and saw what I thought was a nice smooth band of snow rimming the edge of the corrie and leading to the cairn ... I jumped on to it. In an instant I was up to my armpits, and in another instant I had scrambled out on to *terra firma*, considerably frightened ... I had jumped into a small bergschrund (which was covered over with some soft-drifted snow) formed by the shrinking and slipping down of the snow in the corrie ... it gave me a severe fright which I have never forgotten. (Log 1, p10)

– clearly, a man in need of guidance and instruction! (And appropriate behaviour, given the date of the first experience.) But help was at hand, and the next year, on his first SMC meet, he teamed up with the redoubtable Tough, and climbed the 'north-east face' of Ben Lui – presumably the ridge flanking Central Gully. Always one to award praise where due, the Reverend commented,

> This was my first experience of real hard snow and rope work, and I learned much from Tough's excellent skill and guiding. (SMCJ 24, p27)

Exactly one year later he was on another SMC Meet, this time at the Tarbet Hotel and, with a party including the formidable Naismith, did a traverse under winter conditions, of the three peaks of the Cobbler. He observed in the Journal,

The Cobbler, New Year 1931.

It was the best, as well as the most difficult day I had done from a climbing point of view (op.cit. p29)

In his obituary of Maylard, who led the climb, Robertson admitted that he struggled on it, especially on the South Peak, and expressed his gratitude for Maylard's skill and guidance. This traverse, under good conditions a Grade II today, was his pinnacle as a winter climber. Thereafter, though he continued to venture out in winter, and was clearly a competent scrambler on snow and ice, he ventured nothing of such technical difficulty.

A survey of his summer rock-climbing gives a similar picture, although, like many of modest abilities, he was able to do many more rock than snow and ice routes. In the SMCJ (27, 102) he described a 'most enjoyable' climb on the Castle Ridge of Ben Nevis, his second ascent of it, and mentioned the 'ample' holds. Castle Ridge is a Moderate climb, and AER's other solo

scrambling is at roughly the same level. In his fine article *Two Days in Lochaber*, detailing a traverse of the Grey Corries to Ben Nevis, he described the traverse of the Carn Mor Dearg Arête to the Ben. Even allowing for Edwardian hyperbole, the route description is a little overblown,

One of the finest arêtes in Scotland connects Carn Mor Dearg with Ben Nevis. To traverse it is certainly no very easy task, requiring some steadiness of eye, foot and hand. In a high wind its difficulty would be immeasurably increased ... In places the ridge was a true knife-edge, so thin that it was often a matter for speculation on which side an unstable rock would fall if disturbed. (SMCJ 3, p267)

In 1898 AER was at Sligachan Hotel, in the strong company of Parker and the Inglis Clarks. They decided on an ascent of the Pinnacle Ridge of Sgurr nan Gillean. Paired with Inglis Clark, Robertson led the route, finding it to be 'easier than expected' with 'magnificent holds'. He describes the crux,

This descent (from the Third pinnacle) is the *mauvais pas* of the whole climb ... you have to go down ten feet of perpendicular rock on very poor holds. This lands you on a narrow, sloping ledge which ends in a horrid precipice ... (Log 1, p65)

At this point the two gentlemen wait 'to help Mrs Inglis Clark in the descent' – a decision which allows the use of two ropes on the descent of the crux. Pinnacle Ridge is graded Difficult, and it was

Robertson's hardest roped lead as a climber. On the same trip, AER attempted to climb the Bhasteir Tooth, an attempt that failed due to a wind described by Inglis Clark as 'a perfect hurricane' – in June! Robertson was finally to climb it in May 1904 with Kate, and John Mackenzie, the famous Cuillin Guide and friend of Collie.

Tower Ridge from above, c.1902.

Robertson continued to do other climbs, while completing his Munros. In September 1900 in the company of Naismith, he ascended Tower Ridge on Ben Nevis – another Difficult climb – and then the party tried to descend the North-East Buttress. Robertson described what happened,

> After a few hundred feet down, I got off the right route. We fumbled about for a bit, always getting hung up, and so decided to climb back up again to the summit. (SMCJ 24, p85)

It is difficult to think that a climber of Naismith's ability – in reasonable weather – would have problems in descending the North-East Buttress, and we can assume that, like many leaders before or since, he saw that his 'second man' was in difficulty and retreated. Indeed, in his Log, Robertson wrote a passage which he omitted from the published account of this climb.

> I expect it was really my fault and inexperience in mist that I did not hit off the route properly. (Log 2, p24)

On his final trip to complete his Munros, with Sandy Moncrieff and Kate, Robertson had both the peaks of the Aonach Eagach in Glencoe to do. On September 24th 1901 he recorded,

> Fine day. With Kate climbed Sgorr nam Fiannaidh by steep slopes to the east of the big gully. From there we went east along the Aonach Eagach for a bit towards Meall Garbh, but stopped as it was getting rather difficult. (Log 2, p27)

– leaving a separate ascent of Meall Dearg at the east end of the ridge for four days later. Possibly the retreat was out of overprotective Victorian attitudes to the female in the party, but possibly the Reverend, who had scrambled An Teallach solo, found the Aonach Eagach a little daunting.

Robertson's most fruitful period of rock-climbing came after he completed his Munros, when he did several routes at Very Difficult standard, though never leading them. He appears to have had more regular partners, in particular W A Morrison. And indeed, at

The east face of Sgoran Dubh Mor: Rose Ridge is shown by arrows.

this point he had the distinction of participating in a first ascent, and that possibly the most difficult climb he ever did. This was the Rose Ridge, on Sgoran Dubh's Number 2 Buttress. On his second attempt at it, and in a strong party which comprised Newbigging as well as Morrison, they climbed the route on April 29th 1904. The 1961 SMC guide described the route as one of the best climbs on the Gleann Einich face, but the 1985 guide states that Rose Ridge has become dangerously loose. Morrison described the ascent in the SMCJ, and the predicament of the (unnamed) third man on the rope (Morrison himself led the climb),

> After a little (the ridge) narrows down to an arête with one or two very steep pitches up which we swarmed with a leg on each side in a somewhat ungraceful fashion, especially the last man, who, burdened with three ice-axes, found the rope of

more than moral assistance. (SMCJ 8, p154)

The climb continued until a slabby section was reached, followed by a chimney. The hapless third man's situation is portrayed,

> he found the slabs of sufficient difficulty, and on reaching the grassy chimney said in accents doleful, 'Here, give me a haul; I can't get up with all this ironmongery'. (op. cit.)

Could this be Newbigging, a competent climber with several first ascents to his credit? Or is it more than coincidental that the SMC Guide gives the Reverend as the third man on the rope? But nonetheless how lucky he was! At the pioneering stage of Scottish mountaineering, a modest climber could take part in a first ascent of a fine new route. Again we can feel but

Morrison and Newbigging, Rothiemurchus Forest, April 1904.

Goggs, Miss MacDonald and Morrison, Kingshouse, July 1905.

admiration for his pluck, and envy at his opportunity.

Under the guidance of Morrison, Robertson's climbing reached new heights. In 1905 he stayed at the Kingshouse with Morrison and Goggs, and teamed up with another party, including G. Bennet-Gibbs, who described their exploits,

> under the leadership of Morrison, climbed the Crowberry Ridge of Stob Dearg from the slabs at the foot, avoiding Abraham's famous traverse pitch by making use of Maclay's traverse...
> It was agreed with singular unanimity that the pitch is not justifiable for the ordinary run of climbers ... without the slightest possibility of safeguarding the leader after the first few feet. (SMCJ 9, p14.)

The fact that Robertson contemplated this route, done as recently as May 1900 by a very strong party including the Abraham brothers, showed his aspirations

Morrison and Goggs on Abraham's Ledge, Crowberry Ridge, July 1905.

at the time. Defeat possibly sobered him. The fact that the party did not do the leftward traverse, means that the famous photograph of Morrison and Goggs, taken by AER, is a posed one, and that Morrison declined the poorly protected pitch.

A couple of days later, on the 28th of July, they went back to have a second attempt at Church Door Buttress on the Bidean – the proposal to start it at 4.30 pm a few

Diamond and Church Door Buttress, Bidean nam Bian.

days earlier having been vetoed by Goggs and Robertson who did not want to miss dinner! Morrison again led, and on the principle of the more the merrier, the party was expanded to five. They had some difficulty finding their way into the 'Church Door', Bennet-Gibbs commenting 'evidently worshippers are few and far between' from the lack of nail marks.

Church Door Buttress is graded Very Difficult and was another plum route of the period, climbed in July 1898 by a party including J H Bell and Raeburn. This again indicated the Reverend's ambitions, having completed his Munros, to become a rock-climber of merit. But since he had other interests such as photography, possibly he lacked the single-mindedness necessary to progress from the Salvationist ranks to those of the Ultramontanes. After his guided visit to the

Matterhorn in 1908 he appears to have taken little further interest in climbing. He was however fortunate in having been able to climb, albeit at a medium standard, with some of the best climbers of his day, the pioneers of serious Scottish climbing.

Harold Raeburn, 23rd April, 1906.
The greatest Scottish climber of his epoch, photographed the day after he had made the first ascent of Green Gully on Ben Nevis. AER was supposed to have been his partner, but was indisposed, and missed what was the hardest snow and ice climb to that date; one highly rated even today. Next day the pair of them climbed North Castle Gully, where this study was taken.
Raeburn is a study in self-contained precision. Note the formal headwear, the collar and tie, and the handkerchief in the pocket of the well-tailored tweed jacket. Note too the rope coiled in perfect lengths, the good stance, and the geometrically anchored ice-axe.

CHAPTER SEVEN

Transports of Delight

The Reverend Robertson's feat of climbing all the then-known Munros at the beginning of the century was indeed a remarkable one. However, had such a feat been tried – and a list of the 3000 foot peaks been in existence – half a century earlier, then it would have faced greater obstacles to its achievement.

The Reverend was fortunate in that his Odyssey coincided with the opening up of the Highlands for tourism. This meant first of all that he benefited from a transport revolution which facilitated the feat, and secondly from the provision of an infrastructure of accommodation – hotels, and, as we shall see, other habitations, which meant that he could travel light and in a fair degree of comfort.

It is true that in the early nineteenth century this process had started, but it was in its infancy. Read any of the travellers of the time, from Scott to Hogg and Wordsworth, and you will see that their journeys were largely by sail, and later steamer, round the coast of the Highlands and Islands, with forays inland subject to appalling roads and worse hostelries. By the later nineteenth century this had changed. MacBrayne' propeller-driven ships were in command of the high seas off the west coast of Scotland, calling at dozens of locations. The Highland railway system was completed with the opening of the line to Mallaig in 1901 – the Reverend photographed MacAlpine's revolutionary concrete viaduct at Glenfinnan on the line. Fort William was reached in 1894, by a journey of less than 5 hours from Glasgow. Oban itself was but four hours from

Fort William, April 1906.

Glasgow after the railway reached it in 1880. Strome was reached in 1872 (though Kyle not till 1897), as was Wick – and Perth was but a 3 hour journey from Inverness, once Mitchell's line was opened – in 1854! And the system was more extensive than it is today; there was a line to Ballachulish from Oban, and one from Fort William to Fort Augustus. Robertson himself noted in his journal the extension of the railways and photographed the progress of the Iron Horse, including work on one of the final sections of the Mallaig line. And, often forgotten, roads were improving and from around the mid-1890s motor-cars were beginning to be heard in the glens.

But still we keep being told that modern mountaineers are an inferior breed. Told how, in days gone by, the pioneers had it much harder. Told how, with modern transport and all these holidays, mountaineering in Scotland has lost much of the frontier character it had at the start of the century. As

Fort William station, Easter 1929. W Inglis Clark and G T Glover are the two central figures.

early as 1935 J Dow started this myth by stating, 'The ascent of the Scottish Munros under modern transport conditions is very far from being in the slightest degree a feat.' And speaking of the activities of Munro himself and Robertson, Hamish Brown comments, 'It is hard to picture the hills before tarred roads, railways, cars – the things which we all take for granted.' – but the point is, that Munro and Robertson could take many of these things for granted, and some other means of transport little available today.

Let us take the holidays argument first. It is true that most people now (the middle classes and the proletariat) have more holidays than their forebears; maybe five or six weeks in the year, compared with a week or a fortnight before the war. But the mountain pioneers, with whom Robertson mixed, were not 'most people', they were the gentry and the bourgeoisie! Robertson himself took off two periods of three months each to finish his Munros, and this was not simply ministerial good fortune. W Inglis Clark, with whom Robertson climbed was an entrepreneur who could take large periods of time off in summer and winter. Collie was a University professor, who was often – despite his three months holiday – late back from the Himalayas or Canada.

And what about accommodation? Not for the pioneers dirty bothies or the inconvenience of lugging a tent around. People like Munro – a gent himself – often stayed at the seats of the gentry in the mountain areas he visited, for example Inverie House in Knoydart. When times were hard our pioneers roughed it in hotels, like the Alexandra in Fort William, the Kingshouse in Glencoe or the Inveroran. Even off the beaten track they had advantages due to social station – and, admittedly, lack of other visitors. The clearance of the Highlands for sheep and deer was the ill wind that led to the building of remote cottages, from about 1840, for gamekeepers and shepherds, who provided food and shelter for mountaineers.

On Ben Nevis there was a hotel at the top – no need to carry food or sleeping bags – until 1918, long after the Observatory closed. And when the SMC visited Coruisk in 1897 for a pioneering trip, they ferried in enough supplies for a military campaign, and built a village of timber huts for the duration of the Meet!

However, the main argument used by the advocates of the 'sturdy pioneers' view is that of transport. It is true that there were no Ford Sierras for a quick day out up Ben Nevis in those days. But in relation to cars, as early as 1903 Inglis Clark possessed one, and argued that although it could 'cause a degenerate race of mountaineers to arise', it greatly facilitated the sport of

Early mechanised transport for AER – a V-twin Enfield with side-car for Kate.

mountaineering. Though AER did not use a car to complete his Munros, he had access to one for trips to Glencoe by 1906.

The push-bike was in almost universal possession by 1900. These were not the modern mountain bike, true. But remember, many mountain tracks were in better condition then, than now, having been lately drove roads, or roads to shooting lodges for pony and trap. You could cycle to Kinlochquoich easily then; try it now. Many mountain paths were still being maintained, or newly built around the turn of the century, and in some areas going was easier than now – though of course in other places, where Landrover tracks have been bulldozed, going was harder in the past. Robertson makes passing mention in his Log to the question of paths. He notes that a new path has been constructed at Pait Lodge on his great Munro pilgrimage, he observes estate workers repairing the

path near Culra on his first trip to Ben Alder.

> ... I came upon a party of men supposed to be mending the path, but all sound asleep. I gave a shout, and how they jumped up – it afterwards transpired that the proprietor Sir John Ramsden was half-expected up that day. (Log 1, p13)

And the cottage at Ben Alder was reached in those days by a good pony track down Loch Ericht side. Indeed AER observes that Ben Alder is 'engirdled' with 'splendid shooting paths'.

> and by utilising them the tediousness of the long distances to and from the hill is greatly minimised.

Pony and trap bring to mind that before World War One, most hotels had them at the disposal of their guests to take them to the foot of the hills. In addition, there was a regular network of mail coaches (long before post-buses!) that took passengers as well as regular stagecoach services. And who would not now envy Inkson McConnochie, of the SMC and Cairngorm Club, preparing to climb Ben MacDui a hundred years ago in mid-winter, 'The drive from Ballater to Braemar was done on wheels; from Braemar to Derry Lodge it was done in sleighs.'

When hoof and wheel were wanting, there was always ordeal by water. Not only did social contacts give access to the use of gillie-powered boats on Highland lochs, but other means of aquatic propulsion were dragooned into service. When the SMC Easter Meet took place in Knoydart in 1897, they hired a steam yacht, the 'Erne', to ease their access. Steam yachts were stabilised, and equipped with luxuries like billiard rooms. And, of course, the regular steamers made coastal access much

S.S. Clansman

easier than today, calling at most Highland coastal villages and not just main embarkation points. Once the 'Comet' – the world's first steamship – had reached Oban in 1819 from Glasgow, the way was clear for services to the west coast ports. Skye was serviced by regular sailings by 1825 and Stornoway by 1828. By 1880 a fleet of paddle steamers and steamships – largely operated by MacBrayne's – had established a pattern of sailings that was to continue until World War Two, amidst a 'mixed aroma of sheep, kippers and diesel oil' as one traveller put it. By the Reverend's day ships like the 'Clansman' went twice a week from Stornoway to Glasgow, calling at places such as Portree, Broadford, Lochcarron, Kyle, Glenelg, Mallaig, Arisaig, Mull and Oban. What a way to do your mountaineering! (Today the 'Waverley' does the trip – once a year.)

Finally there were the railways, with their sleeping and restaurant cars. These were widely used by the pioneers, and it was the existence of the railway network

that allowed Tough and Brown to do what they thought was the first ascent of North-East Buttress on Ben Nevis, almost exactly a century ago. 'It was arranged that we should travel to Kingussie by the night express on Friday, bicycle to Fort William, and return by the same route on Sunday evening.' In fact, they bicycled to Inverlair on the West Highland line, and entrained again for the Fort. Such a trip would have been impossible without the railway network, and indeed Robertson's achievement in completing the Munros would have been very much harder had he not benefited from these 'transports of delight', and in particular, from the railways. If the internal combustion engine is so today, the steam engine was the transport basis of mountaineering a century ago.

To point out that the undeniably massive achievements of the pioneers of Scottish mountaineering – amongst whom we must consider AER – took place in a context which was more comfortable and less arduous that the romantic mists of hagiography would have us believe, is in no way to belittle their experience: by any criteria and in any context, these achievements were remarkable.

Robertson took full advantage of the revolution in transport which had opened up the Highlands, in his peregrinations of peak-bagging. In one of his first articles for the SMC Journal, 'Two Days in Lochaber', he describes a traverse of the Mamores, Aonachs and Ben Nevis, an area recently opened up by the extension of the West Highland railway. The year was 1893.

> Now that ... the snort of the engine is heard at Roy Bridge in Glen Spean, the wild summits that lie between Fort William and Loch Treig will echo to

Upper Steall, May 1928.

the sound of hobnailers and ice axes ...
(SMCJ 3, p267)

In this article he shows that, not disadvantaged compared with modern mountaineers in terms of transport, he was advantaged in other ways. Today for this walk one would camp or bivouac – for the Reverend there was a more pleasant alternative,

At six o'clock I regained the track, half an hour's walk along which brought me to Steall, a shepherd's house where they readily gave me shelter for the night. (op.cit. p269)

Robertson used the railways to get to his remote bases in the hills, getting off at Dalwhinnie or Rannoch to tramp to McCook's, or at Achnashellach to head for Pait or Strathmore. When on holiday, for example at Loch Awe in 1893, he took a day trip by train to do Stob

Binnein by Crianlarich, and on an SMC Meet at Tarbet the next year he trained to Ardlui for an ascent of Ben Vorlich. The same year the sister hill in Perthshire along with Stuc a' Chroin, was done by train in a day – out from Edinburgh, by another line which no longer, alas, exists,

... some days after this I climbed Ben Vorlich and Stuc a' Chroin from Edinburgh ... I took the early train to Lochearnhead (leaving a bag of dry things at Callander). Then ... to Glen Ample and up by Creagan nan Gabhar to B Vorlich. Down to the bealach between Ben Vorlich and Stuc a' Chroin and, skirting the cliffs I climbed well up the ridge but not quite to the top. Then down ... to a cart track which took me to Callander. There at the hotel I found my bag waiting for me and dinner. I got back to Edinburgh (the) same night. (Log p25)

This trip indicates that day-outing was a pastime not only of the dreaded 1980s, but of the pioneers; the next

Dalnaspidal Station, June 1923. Sow of Atholl behind.

entry in his log shows that by the use of train and steamer Ben Lomond was also 'bagged' on a day trip. They left Glasgow at 8 am, returning exactly 12 hours later after a leisurely day, shipped from Balloch to Rowardennan by steamer in beautifully clear weather, and after a wander up the path to the cairn they were able to discern the new Forth Rail Bridge.

Robertson continued to use the Iron Horse, as for example when he completed his first ascent of Rose Rib with W C Newbigging and W A Morrison. They took the 4.10 am train from Edinburgh to Aviemore, before heading for Glen Einich. Here they were in luck, and utilised a novel and obsolete form of transport up the glen. In those days there were still tree-felling operations in the Rothiemurchus forest. Morrison describes their piece of good luck,

> We had decided not to drive to the Bothy, as the short road was obstructed by a tramway laid to facilitate tree-cutting operations. When we reached the tramway we found the bogie just starting, so promptly seated ourselves thereon and secured a most enjoyable lift, doing the last part at record speed, as our now horseless carriage glissaded down the dip to the cross roads where the tramway ends. (SMCJ 8, p153)

More regular transport was provided by pony and trap, as for example, when AER did Creag Meagaidh,

> On 11th July I left John McLaren's excellent quarters in the well-appointed four-horse coach which every morning passes Moy Hotel on its way from Fort William to Kingussie. Half an hour's smart drive took me down the five miles to Aberarder ... (SMCJ 3, p23)

He also records being 'driven by trap' to do his ascent of Beinn a' Chreachain in 1894; the next year he is taking the 'stage coach to the head of Glen Shiel' and he gets to his headquarters at the Spittal of Glenshee from the railhead at Blairgowrie 'by mail cart'. Clearly, there was no limit to the available 'transports of delight' a hundred years ago!

Over and above giving his readers general comments about the comfort and value of the Highland hostelries – as well as whether or not they were 'temperance', for the Reverend liked his dram – Robertson often glosses his articles with details of the transport facilities available from overnight resting places. Many of them would make the modern mountaineer's heart bleed with envy. This is a note appended to one of the Reverend's guide-book pieces in the SMC Journal (it was actually written by Munro), and shows what was available,

> On Tuesdays a cart capable of taking a bicycle and luggage, but not passengers, is sent up from Glen Affric Hotel, Cannich (no licence) to Beinn Fhionnlaidh Lodge, close to Luib nan Damh, at the west end of Loch Mullardoch in Glen Cannich. The same cart on Thursdays goes up to Glen Affric Lodge. (SMCJ 8, p279)

The availability of a wide selection of means of transport, and of readily available accommodation, meant that on his big trips, Robertson, like Munro before him, could dispense with the need to start and return to the same spot; this gave a wild liberation to his Odysseys that would be difficult to match now. In 'A Tramp through Knoydart and Kintail', described in the SMCJ 3, p351-3, he tells of setting out 'from the Alexandra Hotel' (an SMC favourite) in Fort William and taking 'the Arisaig mail coach' to Glen Finnan. They traverse Sgor Choileam (Sgurr Thuilm?) and descend to Glen Dessary where 'at a large farmhouse ... we asked for and obtained accommodation for the night.' They walk over to Carnach where 'the keeper ... put us up.' They traverse Sgurr na Ciche to Kinlochquoich and another keeper's house, before crossing the mountains to the Shiel Inn in Kintail – which does not earn a rosette from the Reverend – 'Highland charges and very indifferent fare' and the ascent of the Saddle. Finally they walk to Glenelg 'where we caught a homeward-bound steamer.' – this was the 'Clansman', bound for the railhead at Oban.

The minister regularly used steamers to get around the west coast. On his 1898 trip he was driven in a trap from Balmacara to Kyle, where he caught the 'Claymore' to Glenelg, and comments 'slept on board' – steamers, like trains offered accommodation and food as well as transport. We are told, in his guidebook piece on the Saddle (SMCJ 8, p259) that the Shiel Inn 'may be reached by steamer from Glasgow or Oban', and writing of Knoydart, he rather undermines its 'last wilderness' credentials by commenting,

> A small steam launch now runs from Mallaig to Inverie three days a week with the mails, and by arrangement it can be taken to the head of Loch Nevis ... From Inverie, where there is a small but very comfortable temperance inn, a good path goes ... to Carnach, a keeper's house ... (SMCJ 8, p203)

– where, as we know, 'accommodation may be had.'

Other forms of aquatic transport were utilised. Several times Robertson records being rowed across Loch Tulla, from Forest Lodge to Achallader Farm. When at Fannich Lodge in 1898, he is rowed up the loch one day to Sgurr nan Each, and again the next, to Cabuie, for Sgurr Breac and A'Chailleach. But occasionally one can experience a little Schadenfreude at the minister's expense

> On Friday June 1st (1894) I left Edinburgh ... for Dalwhinnie ... intending to stay at Sandy Macpherson's. After a good tea at Loch Ericht Lodge ... I pressed on, intending to hail Sandy for the boat across the loch, but when I reached the spot I found a gale blowing ... which tossed my voice away to nowhere. I roared myself hoarse, but all to no purpose. So I retraced my steps and put up at Loch Ericht Lodge with the Clarks. (Log 1, p25)

But there were many other occasions of compensation. Such as the time in 1901 he crossed and re-crossed Loch Tay from Lawers, *en route* to Ben Chonzie, or when in the same year 'Mr Darroch met us (at Shieldaig) and took us over Loch Torridon to Torridon House' in a boat. Is there anyone so philistine they would not swop the convenience of motorised Munroing for the methods used by AER?

As well as utilising the public transport system, Robertson used his own private transport. The chief of these was the bicycle. In his article 'The 'Munros' of Scotland', he comments,

> The difficulty of getting at the remoter hills, and securing a suitable base of operations was often a very serious one. In this case I found my bicycle simply invaluable, and many of the more distant expeditions ... were brought by the aid of the wheel within the compass of a long day ... One can cycle

up Glen Strathfarrar as far as Monar Lodge, up Glen Cannich as far as the end of Loch Mullardoch, and up Glen Affric as far as Affric Lodge ... (SMCJ 7, p11)

A keen cyclist, Robertson clearly enjoyed combining mountaineering with cycling, and constantly recommends the use of the velocipede in his SMC guide-book contributions. For example, when writing of Ben More Assynt, and remarking on the 'excellent hotel, most comfortable and most moderate,' at Inchnadamph, he observes,

> There is a daily coach from Invershin to Lochinver, passing Inchnadamff, (sic) but a cycle will be found to be at once the more pleasant and the more

Broad Cairn from Capel Mounth.

> independent and expeditious way of getting about in these regions. (SMCJ 6, p36)

And when the Reverend was tramping around with his first wife, Kate, they did so often literally in tandem, having acquired one for the purpose. Further details of his cycling exploits are given in Chapter Four, but particular mention should be made of a Cairngorm cycling marathon in July 1898. He took the train from Balmacara to Grantown-on-Spey, and cycled thence to Inchrory Lodge, where he spent the night. After bagging Beinn a' Bhuird, his log records,

Kate with the tandem.

> Crossed over on bike to Braemar by Loch Builg. This is one of the highest driving roads I know in Scotland. Just to the east of Culardoch it must be over 2500 ft. (Log 1, p72)

He then used Maggie Gruer's at Inverey as a base from which, using his bike, he ticked off his Cairngorm tops, cycling up Glen Ey, the Luibeg and to White Bridge. Thence he cycled to Ballater, at that time the railhead for the Deeside line. If he can be regarded as the father of Munroism, Robertson can also claim to be the founder of the sport of mountain biking. Some might say, he has a lot to answer for!

As far as the use of the motor-car is concerned, the evidence is that Robertson, once he acquired a camera, had access to a car. Indeed many of his slides show cars *en route* to the hills, e.g. in Glencoe or on the way to Mamore Lodge. But when we read his log, it is clear that what he meant by a 'drive' was in a mail coach, dog-cart or similar conveyance. It should be remembered that he only acquired his camera after completing his Munros, and it is unlikely that, had he used the motor-car, he would have failed to mention it in his Log or articles in the SMC Journal. From the charge of being one of the 'degenerate race of mountaineers' feared by Inglis Clark, he can be excused! But just as easily can he be excused from being a sort of Mungo Park in unexplored lands. In many ways his itineraries round the Highlands at the turn of the century were more pleasant, and often more convenient, than those we endure today. One reads his exploits with a mixture of admiration at his determination, and envy at his pioneering good fortune in having the hills largely to himself, and having such a variety of delightful means of access to them.

20 H.P. Austin in Glen Nevis, May 1927 – complete with chauffeur.

CHAPTER EIGHT

Highland Society

As with most visitors, Robertson's experience of Highland culture was selective. Today one can travel the length and breadth of the Highlands, staying in hotels and shopping, and never meet anyone bar a 'white settler' – that is the penalty of being a tourist.

It was different in AER's day but to a certain extent ... *plus ça change.* As a mountaineering tourist Robertson met hoteliers, train guards, ship's crews ... and locals. But the locals he met were largely those he sought accommodation from; shepherds and gamekeepers, the residual legatees of the Clearances, and not 'traditional' Highlanders in a social context. There is nothing in Robertson's Log about meetings with the crofter-fishermen of the Western Highlands, since by and large these groups did not live where they could be of use to his mountaineering exploits. In his writings there is no reference to the Clearances – though their relics were still everywhere visible – and none to the recent Crofters' War. As a tourist he had little interest in the social and economic problems of the Highlander at a time of acute economic and social crisis. Thus it is not strictly accurate to say, as Bell does in the already-cited obituary that Robertson knew the language and the people of the western Highlands.

We have already discussed the Reverend's grasp of Gaelic, which he made a serious effort to learn. And, though he probably met an unrepresentative cross section of Highlanders, he had a sympathetic attitude to those he encountered. He displayed a typical paternalistic view of the Highlanders, evident when he discusses Knoydart as,

one of the few districts not yet corrupted by the monied Sassenach, and the people of the glen, not being spoiled by the vulgar products of modern civilisation, are kind, courteous and hospitable. (SMCJ 8, p206)

Robertson was like his contemporary mountaineers, in that they assumed that, if they turned up at a shepherd's or keeper's cottage, they would be given accommodation – though he does caution that one should ask politely. This undoubtedly reflects the patriarchal confidence of the Victorian and Edwardian upper classes, that the lower classes would be, literally, accommodating. His guide-book entries abound with references to cottages where 'accommodation may be had' – Camban, Gorton, Oban, Glendessary amongst others.

Camban, May 1906.

From the latter in 1895, AER and some companions set out to climb Sgurr na Ciche. The Reverend's Log comments,

A magnificent cone-shaped hill faced us at the head of the glen ... We made for it ... I discovered to my intense disgust and the amusement of Sandy and

Mirylees, that we were not on Sgurr na Ciche at all. (Log 1, p33)

However, in the official account of the trip, published in the SMCJ, the Reverend indulges in a bit of poetic licence,

> Next morning we continued on our way up Glen Dessary. A very high hill ... Sgurr na h-Aide so attracted our attention that we determined to set foot on it. (SMCJ 3, p351)

What did St. Peter have to say about this mismatch between personal log and official account? But let the Reverend continue the tale,

> We took our way down a path to Loch Nevis, where from Sgurr na h-Aide we had seen some cottages where we hoped to obtain quarters for the night. The near view of them did not greatly please us. They were dirty, damp and badly thatched ... However, any port in a storm, and so I knocked on the door of one of them. Imagine our surprise when out stepped a Highlander in full Highland costume; kilt, cap, shoes. I believe he even had a dirk ... It was like stepping back into the days of the '45 ... We told him our tale. 'Perhaps the keeper at Carnach will put you up. Here he is.' One or two other men emerged from sundry peat-smoked dwellings and a prolonged dispute arose amongst them in Gaelic. At last the keeper came forward and told us that we were welcome to whatever we could find in the way of food and hospitality. 'I have only one bed and there are three of you, but you will have to make the best of it.' ... (Mirylees) pulled a long 'kist' along the bed and re-made the bed across it. Thus three slept transversely in the bed – very comfortable too! (Log 1, p33–4)

This is a fascinating extract. One would like to know what was said in the Gaelic conversation – Robertson clearly could not follow it. There is a suspicion of a certain lack of enthusiasm amongst the Highlanders for their unbidden guests. It is not mentioned where the keeper slept – presumably on the floor – nor whether he was paid for his trouble. Only once does Robertson mention payment for such accommodation – when he stays two weeks with Kate at McCooks, and this from a man who rigorously recorded in his diary the price of every haircut he had! AER was undoubtedly no different from the other gentleman climbers of his time in the assumptions that he made in such contexts. Indeed, it is the very fact that he was typical that makes him interesting.

As he matured, Robertson grew more and more interested in the history of the lands he tramped. His *Old Tracks and Coffin Roads* pamphlet is full of fascinating details and observations of the kind which are missing from the Log he wrote of his Munroing expeditions. There are, of course, the obligatory references to the wanderings of Bonnie Prince Charlie, on which AER became something of an expert, contributing an article on that topic to the SMC *Western Highlands* guide-book. And there is information on the iron workings at Kinlochewe, about quaint Highland burial customs, and the explanation of the existence of the 'soldiers' trenches' on the Rannoch Moor. He describes illicit smuggling at Loch Monar, where are to be found 'the ruins of Jamie MacRae's smuggling bothies'. (When things got too hot, MacRae betrayed his own stills to the gaugers and pocketed the reward.) And of course, AER displays his greatest erudition on the historical background to the roads he is discussing.

But it is still a tourist's Highlands that the Reverend deals with; there is no reference to the wealth of Gaelic culture – poem, story and song – in his writings, nor to any of the more modern manifestations of the Gael's culture such as his politics or his religion. One suspects that AER would have been uneasy with the radical Liberal politics of the Highlander, as with his Free Church enthusiasm, and happier with the isolated and deferential keepers and shepherds who gave him shelter in their lonely cottages in the glens. As with so many other things, Robertson's interactions with those Highlanders he met give a fascinating insight into the period.

Jamie and Mary MacRae, West Monar.

CHAPTER NINE

Access to the hills

The opening up of the Highlands by the transport revolution we have outlined earlier made Robertson's achievement in climbing all the Munros possible. It also removed the barriers to an influx, first of casual tourists, and then avowed mountaineers, into the glens and onto the bens. But the removal of barriers to access also caused a revolution in land use in the Highlands, which posed problems as well as opportunities for the early climbers.

The chronically underdeveloped Highland economy had gone through crisis after crisis since 1745. At first the bankrupt and indebted landlords had attempted to clear the land of people and replace them with sheep. This phase lasted from about 1750 until around the mid-nineteenth century, and was marked by many cruelties, such as the evictions by Patrick Sellar in Sutherland. But a decline in the profitability of sheep farming, coupled with the increasing sporting opportunities offered by the Highlands (opportunities for fishing, grouse-shooting and most notably for deer-stalking) led in the next half-century to a rapid switch from sheep to deer. Rents of estates like Glenmoriston rose from £100 a year in 1835 to £3000 in 1872 with the switch. The result was that by 1914 some 20% of Scotland, amounting to three and a half million acres in the Highlands, was under deer forest or grouse moor.

The problems this caused for the Highlanders were evictions, which should be borne in mind by those who wax eloquent about 'wilderness' Scotland and its splendid isolation. But the situation also caused

problems for the new breed of mountaineer, a casual visitor before 1880, but increasingly frequent thereafter with the formation of the SMC, Cairngorm Club and so forth. Basically the problem was this. Before the mid-century the right to free access in Scotland was generally recognised; landlords had no reason to oppose it in the economically sterile countryside in the Highlands. In particular the old drove roads which ran through the glens were open to all; the economic interest of the landlord necessitated their use to transport first cattle then sheep to the southern markets. The additional odd traveller, such as Burns or Hogg, was untroubled.

But with the development of deer forest all this changed. In the first place walkers and climbers could disturb the shoot and thus lose business for the landowner. But deer-stalking was also the sale of a life style which depended for its marketability on exclusiveness and the Victorian cult of the Arcadian countryside. To the Victorian upper middle class this meant no Highland peasants and no damned walkers or climbers! Thus a systematic campaign to close the glens and remove access to the hills was begun – often by industrialists like Baird who purchased Knoydart, often by foreign owners who bought up estates for speculation even in those days, often by the residual legatees of the clan chiefs. This took the form of occasional force-armies of gillies blocking access to paths and peaks, and to the frequent use of legal interdicts and prosecutions of walkers. When John Stuart Blackie climbed the Buachaille in 1867, he was given a glass of port by the fiscal in Fort William and told that the landowner had instructed that he be prosecuted.

One of the worst offenders was the Duke of Athole,

whose gillies forcibly prevented access to Glen Tilt, and who himself assaulted the Provost of Perth who was active in the access battle. The well known Battle of Glen Tilt was the upshot, where a party of Edinburgh botanists, led by Professor Balfour forced access and subsequently won a legal battle that established access in the glen. And that was the problem. In each case access had to be fought for and the traditional use – and continued use – of the road be proven. It was to forward this battle that the Scottish Rights of Way Society was founded in 1845. Attempts to have a general law of access, with rights to roam off the path, were repeatedly made by James Bryce, Liberal MP for South Aberdeen, first president of the Cairngorm Club and one-time president of the Alpine Club, but he got little support in the landlord-influenced Commons, and indeed, little support from the various Scottish climbing clubs, including the Cairngorm Club.

The reasons for this are complex. It is a contributory, but not sufficient factor, to point out that many of the early mountaineers were themselves landowners, (Munro of the SMC being the prime example) and the Cairngorm Club counted Grant of Monymusk as one of its elect. But a majority of the early climbing club activists were members of the urban bourgeoisie and the professional classes, not landowners. Why was it that though a few SMC and Cairngorm Club members joined and supported rights of way agitation, the majority – and their clubs – did not?

A further reason, suggested by Robert Aitken in his amusing *Stravagers and Marauders* (SMCJ 30, p351) is that most of the SMC members were in the Alps in the summer and only on the Scottish hills outside the stalking season, and then often on hills like the Cobbler,

that were not deer forest. He suggests the non-Alpine and deer-forest tramping Cairngorm Club were more radical, citing the activities of Alexander Copland, its Chairman. But this argument is flawed. Landowners tried to ban access at all times, not just the late-summer shoot, and Glencoe and Nevis – SMC stomping grounds – were deer forest at that time, though no longer so today. And the Cairngorm Club was hardly more radical than the SMC, despite being possibly more Liberal rather than Tory in its composition. Whilst in 1878 Copland expressed the outright, radical view that;

> Our native Mumbo Jumbos who molest the traveller in Glen Derry, Glen Lui Beg, and other wilds ... selfishly, out of excessive zeal for shooting deer, seek to prevent the inhabitants of this country from visiting its finest scenery ... It is intolerable that this should be permitted.

eleven years later it seems that the turmoil produced by the Irish Land League had influenced his public attitude. Then the Aberdeen Journal of 23rd Sept. 1889 quoted from his speech on the top of Lochnagar, at the Club's second meet that the Club does not wish,

> to interfere with or usurp the rights and property of the proprietors of this or any other country. We are not Revolutionists, but loyal and law-abiding subjects: we are not enemies of game or legitimate sports ... There need be no friction between us and the proprietors of the land, on the contrary ... (The Cairngorm Club: Sheila Murray p13).

And here we have it; 'revolutionists'! The time of these access conflicts was the time of the Fenian-inspired land war in Ireland. It was a time of the Crofters' War and agitation for Highland land rights, stirred up amongst others by Murdoch in Inverness in his paper the 'Highlander', and by such as Blackie – the trespasser on the Buachaille! The staunchly loyal Tory or Liberal members of the Club wished to strongly dissociate their activities from any suspicion of an attack on property rights. Nationalisation of the land had already been demanded by Henry George, and by the early forerunners of the Labour party, the ILP and SDF, thus posing a threat to landed property rights.

And what of the SMC? Many members like Parker Smith and Munro dissociated themselves from Bryce's attempts to legalise access rights, as did the SMC President Ramsay, who commented,

> I and my friends had no desire to see the proposed Club mixed up in any attempt to force rights of way. We did not desire the Club to become a stravaging or marauding Club, insisting on going everywhere at every season ... (SMCJ 4, p88)

The SMC favoured a policy of amicable agreement with landowners, politely requesting access for their own small numbers at times convenient to the lairds. The policy was quoted in all SMC guides,

> It is essential at all times to respect proprietary and sporting rights, especially during the shooting season, and to avoid disturbing game in deer forests and grouse moors. (Western Highlands Guide, 1931 ed., p136)

This then was the background to the access question when Robertson took up mountaineering and joined the SMC. However, given the Club's cautious attitude on the question of access, we should not expect Robertson to be a firebrand on the access question. In his article 'The Munros of Scotland', he comments,

> In the interests of sporting rights, most, if not all the hills under deer were climbed either in spring or early summer. (SMCJ 7, p13)

It is also worth pointing out that the legal issue of access in Scotland was – and is – shrouded in obscurity. The origin of Scotland's more liberal system of access (than England's) is debateable. As the Society itself said in the 1979 edition of the 'Walkers' Guide to the Law of Rights of Way in Scotland',

> There has been considerable judicial discussion as to whether all rights of way have their ultimate origin in an implied grant by the proprietor, but the question is largely an academic one. (p7)

The de facto position appears to be that pedestrians and possibly cyclists have legal access to rights of way paths, and cannot be prosecuted for trespass if they stray off them, only for any damage committed. And while it also appears that a proprietor has the right to request a walker to leave his land – other than a right of way – the use of force to achieve this can be construed as assault. Thus Scotland has neither the English system of trespass law, nor the Scandinavian system of unlimited access, though nearer to the latter. Robertson summed up the assumed legal position in 1944, in an article for the 'Scottish Geographical Magazine',

> Simple trespass in Scotland, i.e. walking about on somebody's land without a gun or a rod, is not a criminal offence ... The sign TRESPASSERS WILL BE PROSECUTED is an empty threat. What the owner of the ground can do is to proceed against you in the civil courts ... He cannot lay violent hands on you. If he does and you have a witness to support you, he lays himself open to a charge of assault.

A misleading notice. Fannich road, Easter 1935.

Robertson was in many ways typical of his historical period and social class in his attitudes. But he was atypical of most of his fellow gentlemen mountaineers in being prepared to take up the cudgels against the landowners on behalf of climbers and walkers, and he became involved in the Scottish Rights of Way Society, to the extent of becoming its Chairman in the 1930s.

CHAPTER TEN

AER and Rights of Way

The Scottish Rights of Way Society fought several issues of access as old drove roads were closed in the later nineteenth century. For example in the 1880s they waged a successful case against the new owner of Glen Doll, Duncan MacPherson, who had closed the glen to drovers and walkers. (*Battles for Cairngorm Rights of Way* Sandy Anton CCJ 1991)

But in 1894 responsibility for the maintenance of rights of way was vested in Town and County Councils by the Local Government (Scotland) Act. This led to a decline in the activity of the Society, which only had two meetings between 1898 and 1923! At one of these it was commented, 'The Society has not the same work and responsibility as formerly.' 13.7.04 (GD 335 61)

But with the situation after the First World War and the influx of new owners to Highland estates – many from overseas and ignorant of Scots legal practice – with the expansion of the Hydroelectric schemes from 1920 onwards, and the activities of the Forestry Commission, a plethora of new cases arose. Thus the Society was revived, having its first meeting on 15th March 1923. An account of this meeting was quoted in the 'Scotsman' of 29.3.23, giving expression to sentiments of which doubtless the Reverend would have approved,

> We are not a revolutionary body wanting to take anything from proprietors. We are strictly conservative, in wishing to conserve for the public what belongs to them.

One of the issues which had led to the revival was the Glentanar case where Lord Glentanar, the proprietor, had attempted to block the right of way in the glen by 'great gates which are shut at night' as well as by moving families from the glen.

With the help of the Aberdeen County Council, the Society fought the case, which was eventually decided in its favour. Although Robertson had been elected as a director of the Society on 28th March 1923, and was a regular attender at its meetings at this time, he played no role in this case, possibly as it lay in an area he had little knowledge of. He does not appear to have revisited the Cairngorms after completing his 'Munros'.

So what kind of work did AER do for the society? First as a director and from 1931 as Chairman, it was as indefatigable as it was routine. Much of the work of the Society and AER was taken up with the placing of signposts, negotiation about locked gates, donations for the construction and repair of bridges. For example, when the old Glencoe road was closed. The minutes of the Society record that,

> The Reverend A E Robertson stressed the importance, in regard to the Glencoe road, of preserving the existing right of way from Inveroran Hotel by Barr (sic) Bridge to Kingshouse, and moved that the Society should endeavour to see that the right of way is preserved. (61, p285)

He himself visited Blackmount estate to negotiate the unlocking of gates and placing of signposts on the old military road. An SMC Journal correspondent, reporting on the 1935 Kinlochewe meet, had a gentle dig at these activities of his:

AER, Easter 1935: rights of way activist.

Robertson spent the day wandering over the Coulin Forest at the same time as Ling, Glover, Unna and Anderson, on their way from Achnasheen, were saying hard things about the Chairman of the Scottish Rights of Way Society and the inaccuracy of some of his signposts. (SMCJ 20, p440)

The Society also wrote to landowners regarding misleading signs – often without avail,

The Chairman referred to the existence of so many misleading notices throughout the country. These 'Private Road' notices ... were difficult for the Society to deal with. (62, p126)

Despite his high office in the Society – in 1946 he was elected Honorary President – Robertson's role was never really to the forefront of combativeness. The one post he never occupied was that of secretary, dealing with correspondence, complaints, negotiation with landowners, and thus there is relatively little in the Society's records in his hand. Apart from attendance at meetings, his main role was as a sort of elder statesman, being consulted by the Society on legal and historical aspects of rights of way. He also mapped out all the 'deemed' rights of way on Bartholomew quarter-inch maps for their records, and occasionally visited problem landowners on behalf of the Society. They obviously saw him as a good bet for buttering up the proprietors!

An example of this was after the Second World War, when – though he started dropping out of meetings – being replaced almost permanently from 1954 by his wife Winifred, Robertson took an active part in attempting to limit the damage to rights of way from the massive expansion of hydroelectricity in the Highlands. In October 1951, for example, the minutes record that,

The President reported briefly on a recent visit he had made to the Hydro Electric Scheme in Glen Affric and Glen Cannich. On his suggestion it was agreed that the secretary should write to the Hydro Electricity Board and remind them of their undertaking to construct new paths where necessary, and in particular to make a new track alongside Loch Mullardoch. (63, p151)

– today, we are still waiting!

Robertson believed in publicity rather than confrontation, as the means of preserving rights of way. He argued that, 'there was always a conspiracy of silence on the part of landowners, factors and Local Authorities' in the Highlands about rights of way, as opposed to the Lowlands and Borders, where they upheld their statutory obligations, and he blamed this on the domination of local politics by the landowners – how this squared with his Tory politics is difficult to ascertain. It was this that decided Robertson to publish his most successful pamphlet, *Old Tracks, Cross Country Routes and Coffin Tracks in the North West Highlands* in 1941, publicising many of the more and less famous routes in the area. Concerning it he comments,

> Ignorance is what some of the Highland proprietors and many of their factors count on. 'You know too much, Mr Robertson,' said a well-known factor playfully to me one day in Inverness. 'What I would like to do to you is to stick a knife in your ribs and tumble you into a peat hole, and then all the information you have would perish with you.' It is to help to combat that eventuality that this article has been written!...
> ...and it is up to the walking public and hikers and hill walkers to traverse these roads and not to be daunted by misleading signposts.
> 'Private Road' is one of the commonest of these.
> (SMCJ 22, p327–8)

Apart from all this very necessary but rather undramatic work for the Society, Robertson was involved in what was – with the Glentanar Case – the longest and most difficult dispute between the Society and a landowner between the wars. Although this one did not come to civil disobedience – there was no Scottish Kinder Scout – or even to a court case, it is well to go into it in some detail, as it typifies the moderate attitude of the Society towards the issue of

Path on north side of Loch Coulin, Easter 1935.

access and disputes with landowners.

The Coulin Pass, between Torridon and Achnashellach was an ancient right of way and drove road. In the early 1930s a new owner of the Coulin estate, Lord Davies, denied the existence of such a right of way, and correspondence passed between himself and George Cheyne, secretary of the Society, on the issue throughout 1932 (Rights of Way File No 127 'Achnashellach to Kinlochewe'). Soon acrimonious letters were passing between Cheyne and Mr Borthwick the factor of the estate and the issue dragged on till 1934, when in a letter to E P Campbell who had complained of being barred from the road, Cheyne wrote (24.6.34)

> this year evidently, instructions have been given to turn people from using the present road.

adding that he had received two other complaints on the

case. Cheyne handled all the correspondence on the issue, and reported regularly to the Society on the progress – or lack of it – over the dispute. What then was the Reverend's role? Early on in the exchange Robertson was asked for a submission on the legal and historical aspect of the Coulin case, and this he presented to the Society on October 11th 1932. In this detailed submission (File 127 in AER's handwriting), he firstly describes the historical route from Achnashellach to Kinlochewe, as a 'natural and direct' route in use 'from the earliest of times'. He then points out that it is marked as a road on Roy's Military Survey of 1747–54, and that Hogg, the Ettrick shepherd, walked the road in 1803. He then adds that he had cycled the route in 1905, being given to understand by another local proprietor, Duncan Darroch of Torridon House, that the road was a right of way, and says that 'Mr Darroch was a very particular man and most correct in his attitude to neighbouring proprietors.'

He records that in the summer of 1932 he had revisited the area, interviewing locals such as Farquar MacDonald, who remembered cattle being driven over the road, and a Sandy Mackenzie, who recalled the road as a coffin track where funerals might be halted by snow but not a lack of a right of way. Robertson concludes,

> All this surely points to the fact that the road has been long used by all and sundry going on their lawful occasions from Kinlochewe to Strathcarron.

Such information was invaluable to Cheyne, and its use did much to convince the estate to come to a compromise with the Society – and here again the Reverend was wheeled into action. As Chairman, he met Borthwick sometime between the 2nd and 8th of July 1934, and a new route was agreed, without the estate having conceded the legality of the old route.

Basically this new route took the path well away from Coulin House and the general policies of the owner. Robertson wrote an article for the SMC Journal, outlining the new route and commenting favourably on the arrangement.

> By this arrangement the private policies of Coulin Lodge are left undisturbed, and the public get a route which is quite clear, and good going all the way ... cyclists are warned that they will have to be prepared to wheel their cycles along the track between Torran Coulin and Kinlochewe ... the way of leave for pedestrians which (Coulin Estates) have granted as a quid pro quo ... is of great benefit to the walking public.

In fact, the estate gained more, by moving an undisputed right of way, to a more convenient location to the owner. For his work, AER earned the merited plaudits of the Society,

> The Chairman was cordially thanked for the trouble he had taken in obtaining evidence of the old right of way and for negotiating with Mr Borthwick. (62 p87)

The Coulin case is a fine example of the work of the Society, with its insistence on public access, combined with respect for proprietorial rights, leading to a policy of negotiation and compromise, rather than confrontation. As well as insisting on the limitations of access, e.g. to cycles, the Society was quite traditional in its attitudes in other ways. This was the time of the early proletarian revolution, of the unemployed of the cities discovering the countryside. Now, while undoubtedly the Reverend would have approved of this, his approval would have been on the basis of such activities being channelled through such organisations as the recently-founded Youth Hostels association. A little gem found in the minutes of the Society actually deals with one of these manifestations of anarchic proletarian behaviour – and the horror of the Reverend at it.

> Mr Ferris reported on an obstruction by a group of campers lighting fires and camping on the path. It was agreed that the secretary should write to the Chief Constable of Stirling complaining on the use made of the path. (62, 115–6 'Craigallion Loch' 5.9.35)

This was a meeting chaired by Robertson and, of course, the Society is sending the long arm of the law against the early Creag Dhu, typical of the growing band of mountaineers who took rather than asked for access. One wonders in the end whether the ordinary mountaineer just going and doing did as much to wear down the resistance of the lairds, as all the negotiations of the Rights of Way Society.

A spin-off from AER's work with the Rights of way Society was his attitude to conservation of the Scottish wilderness. The Reverend was no John Muir. However, examination shows that in his later years he was prepared to envisage some restrictions being placed on land ownership in the interests of conservation.

What is noticeable about Robertson and his companions at the turn of the century is their complacency about the environment, doubtless an aspect of the general Victorian-Edwardian middle class complacency about life in general; things were, largely for the best, is clearly their attitude. As we have already indicated, there was no criticism of the use of the Highlands as deer forest, a practice whose environmental consequences were already apparent. When Robertson and his companions are in Glen Einich, they observe forestry operations, felling Scots Pine, without comment. The pictures he took of Barrisdale Bay or Coire Ardair when the tree cover was much greater than now show the relentless effect of over-grazing by deer or sheep, or the felling of pines for pit-props and ammunition boxes in the First World War. These things we can see with the benefit of hindsight, and while it would be unfair to criticise AER for not seeing them, it is worth pointing out that the issue of 'conservation' did not seem to exist for him and his peers at the turn of the century.

His few random observations on the environment in his writings are generally about litter (and even then, hardly helpful!), as when he climbs Castle Ridge on Ben Nevis,

> I was much shocked at the mess everything was in around the abandoned Observatory ... All around outside is a confused jumble of rotten wood, rusty corrugated iron, broken glass et hoc genus omne ... I would like to organise a summer fatigue party of the S.M.C. and pitch all the loose rubbish down Gardyloo Gully! (SMCJ 17, p103)

The increased use of the mountains by the growing

numbers of outdoor enthusiasts between the wars, as well as his conflicts with the landed interest through his work with the Rights of Way Society stimulated him into wider consideration of land use, and he was the Rights of Way representative on the Scottish Council for National Parks, and produced reports for the Society on how the idea of national parks was progressing. Robertson supported the idea of the acquisition of land for National Parks by the new National Trust for Scotland, with restriction on developments on designated land along the lines proposed by Percy Unna, one of the Trusts's main benefactors, whose grants enabled the Trust to buy – inter alia – Glencoe. Robertson favoured restrictions of camping, road-making and construction in the proposed National Parks, commenting in his report to the Society,

to merely schedule an area leaving it in the possession of a private owner, subject to unrestricted access by the public, would not be satisfactory. (GD 335, p330)

Given the wider ecological and environmental awareness of today, the Reverend's proposals may seem modest. But when we consider the class and period he came from it is clear he was in advance of most of his peers in fighting both for access to the Highlands, and for some restrictions on the right of private landowners to inflict damage to the natural heritage, and for that he deserves our thanks.

Part Three:

*Old tracks, cross-country routes and coffin roads in the North-West Highlands

Information about the cross-country routes and coffin roads in the Highlands will, in coming years, be of increasing interest and value to those who want to leave the tar-mac and feel the heather under their heel – getting away from the crowds and the stir of modern urban life. In the course of my misspent life I have picked up a considerable amount of such information, and it is but right that this should be set down on paper, else some of it might be lost.

Ignorance is what some of the Highland proprietors and many of their factors count on. "You know too much, Mr Robertson," said a well-known factor playfully to me one day in Inverness. "What I would like to do to you is to stick a knife in your ribs and tumble you into a peat hole, and then all that information you have would perish with you." It is to help to combat that eventuality that this article has been written! The public have the right to use these old paths and drove roads and coffin roads, no man making them afraid; and, so long as they do not blaze their trail with litter and empty tins and broken bottles, I say "God speed them."

A right-of-way has to be used unless it is to lapse (disuse for fifty years constituting a lapse), and it is up to

* First published simultaneously in the Scottish Mountaineering Club Journal and as a separate pamphlet in 1941. The pamphlet was reprinted five times.

the walking public and hikers and hill-walkers to traverse these roads and not be daunted by misleading signposts.

'Private Road' is one of the commonest of these. It may be that the owner of the land has constructed at his own expense a motor road for his own use along the line of part of an old drove road, but, while this road may be 'private' as far as motors are concerned, it does not debar the walking public from going over it. The route was a right-of-way long before the 'private' motor road was made over it.

Poolewe to Kinlochewe

Let me begin by describing the old post road and line of communication from Poolewe to the east and south. Poolewe, before Oban and Mallaig came into being, was a very important harbour and place of call in the north-west. The packet boats carrying the mails for Lewis and Stornoway started from it, and foreign vessels with goods and contraband from the Low Countries and elsewhere used it. Prince Charlie, skulking in the Highlands after Culloden in 1746, sent messengers from Glen Cannich to Poolewe for tidings of a French vessel which might be cruising about in the hope of picking him up. It was by this route I am about to describe that these messengers undoubtedly went. Starting from Poolewe it goes eastwards to Kernsary, then south by the west side of Loch Tholldhoire to the shores of Loch Maree at Ardlair, and along through the rocky slopes of Creag Tharbh (the Bull Rock) to Letterewe. The late Mr Osgood Mackenzie in his book, *A Hundred Years in the Highlands*, in Chapter III. gives a vivid description of the 'perils' of this bit of the road. From Letterewe it keeps mostly near the shores of the loch past Furnace to Kinlochewe, a rough track but fairly distinguishable all the way. Over two hundred years ago the woods on this side of the loch were cut down for the smelting of iron ore: and the bloomeries are still here and there traceable.

Please do not make this path a jumping-off place at Glen Bannisdale to go up the Glen *en route* for Slioch in the shooting season. It is one of the best beats in the Kinlochewe Forest, and it is hardly fair to disturb it.

Kinlochewe is a name of comparatively recent origin. There is no mention of it in General Roy's Military Map, 1747-55, but the names of three hamlets are given – Rinach, Bord, and Froskans. Rinach is where the existing ancient graveyard stands; Bord is the site of the old change-house beside a small modern merchant's shop; and Froskans stood across the river near the present Parish Church.

From Kinlochewe a very old and interesting right-of-way goes north-east to the 'Heights of Kinlochewe,' then up the Gleann na Muice to an old ruined bothy, then over the Bealach na Croise by Loch an Nid and the head of Strath na Sheallag to Dundonnell. One mile south of Loch an Nid a branch track goes off east by Loch a' Bhraoin to Braemore and Ullapool. This, in reverse direction, was the route that Lord Louden and Principal Forbes of Culloden with about eight hundred men took in their retreat from Dornoch to Skye in March 1746 to avoid being captured by Prince Charlie's troops. They came up Strath Oykell to Oykell Bridge, then turned down Glen Einig, Loch na Daimh, and by Rhidorroch to Loch Broom. That day they reached Kinlochewe, so it must have been by the route south through the hills that they travelled; thereafter they went by the Coulin Pass to Loch Carron and so to Skye.

This is a very interesting sidelight on the use made of these cross-country routes two hundred years ago, and on horseback too! Louden and Forbes undoubtedly would be riding, not to speak of many of the eight hundred men with them. *For an account of this episode consult 'More Culloden Papers,' Vol. 5, p. 47 and following.*

Kinlochewe to Coulin and Strath Carron
Carrying on southwards by the Poolewe line of communication to the Lowlands, the route goes up the east bank of the Allt Ghairbh at Kinlochewe (a gateway on the main road just beside the Parish Church giving access to the track). At first for about a mile or so the path is fairly distinct, but when it begins to slope upwards over the north-west side of Carn Dhomhnuil Mhic a' Ghobha it fades away in parts, going over rough and boggy ground. It becomes clearer and better nearing Torran-cuilinn. Here you cross the river by a footbridge and reach the 'private' motor road which has been constructed along the line of the old right-of-way. It is now good going across the Easan Dorcha stone bridge made by the late Lord Leeds when the Dingwall and Skye railway came into being, and on over the Coulin Pass to Achnashellach Station. Before the days of the railway the drove road descended steeply from the Pass to Craig, the old inn and stance. Near where the Easan Dorcha Bridge now stands the path in the old days divided; one branch going north by Torran-cuilinn to Kinlochewe, the other by the south-west side of Loch Clair and Loch Bharranch to Torridon. This path went through the private policies of Coulin Lodge, which meant a certain amount of disturbance and unpleasantness. Accordingly, some years ago the Scottish Rights-of-Way Society took the matter up, and

an arrangement was made whereby wayleave was granted from Torran-cuilinn along the north side of Loch Coulin and Loch Clair to the main road in Glen Torridon. By this arrangement the private policies of Coulin Lodge are left undisturbed and the public are given a clear route, the scenic qualities of which are unsurpassed. In this connection let me advise all pedestrians going to Kinlochewe from Torran-cuilinn to take the path by Loch Coulin and Loch Clair to the Glen Torridon road, thence along it to Kinlochewe. Avoid the old route by Carn Dhomhnuil Mhic a' Ghobha, which, although it may be a little shorter, is a very fatiguing route. Contrariwise, when going from Kinlochewe to Torran-cuilinn I strongly advise taking the Glen Torridon road to Loch Clair, and thence by the good path along the north side of Loch Coulin. It is one of the most beautiful walks in the Highlands. It is interesting to note that James Hogg, the Ettrick Shepherd, explored this region in 1803, and he describes his experiences in a series of letters to Sir Walter Scott. They were reprinted in a small volume entitled "A Tour of the Highlands in 1803," by Alex. Gardner, Paisley, 1888, and are well worth perusal. He had walked from Lochaber by Glen Garry, Loch Duich, and Strath Carron. He reached Craig expecting to be put up for the night, but he could only get whisky. The master and mistress were away, leaving girls in charge who had no English. As Hogg had no Gaelic the situation became perplexing and difficult, and it ended in Hogg taking the Coulin route, late in the day, and reaching Kinlochewe very hungry and tired. His whole account of his travels is very vivid and interesting and well worth reading.

Strath Carron to Monar, Cannich, Tomich, Fort Augustus

There is now no inn at Craig, but a very well-equipped and much-frequented Youth Hostel is near at Achnashellach. The right-of-way crosses the railway here (gates and even side gates being provided for the passage of the droves); it then follows a very rough motor road which has been made along the line of the old track up the Allt a Chonais to Glenuaig Lodge. From the Lodge the way is clear into Strath Conon by the River Meig. By this way Principal Forbes of Culloden travelled from Skye to Inverness in April 1746 (vide *'More Culloden Papers,' Vol. 5, p.64*). The south-going route, however, breaks off a little to the west of Glenuaig Lodge and goes up the Crom-allt and down by the side of Loch Mhuilich to the west end of Loch Monar, thence east along the loch side by Lub an Inbhir to East Monar. At Inchvuilt it crosses the River Farrar at a ford just above the present wooden bridge, and then takes the hillside through the wood, gradually rising to the Bealach between Meall an Odhar and An Soutar and down the burnside to Liatrie in Glen Cannich. It was hereabout that Prince Charlie waited for the return of the messengers he had sent to Poolewe for tidings, 5th to 7th August 1746. It is now a good road down Glen Cannich to Strath Glass and up by Fasnakyle to Tomich. From Tomich it is only a track going up past the Guisachan farm-steading to the high ground above Hilton Cottage and up the Eas Socach along the east side of Loch na Beinn Baine, following hard ground in a winding course on the west side of Beinn Bhreac and Meall na Doire to Torgyle in Glen Moriston, close to the little R.C. Church. You then cross the Torgyle Bridge and go due south from the end of the bridge joining the old military road which is followed down to Fort Augustus. From Fort Augustus the route to the south climbs over the Corrieyairack to Laggan and Dalwhinnie – a well-used track which need not be described here. It may be recorded that Lord Tweedmouth and Mr Winans had a lawsuit in 1888 over the rights-of-way in Guisachan. The Court of Session declared the track from Tomich to Torgyle and from Tomich to Corrimony to be rights-of-way (vide *'General Collection of Session Papers,' 1888, 7th February to 10th March*).

Glen Strath Farrar to Kintail

Now to describe some little-known routes branching off to the west of the Poolewe-Fort Augustus line of communication. There is a very important right-of-way and coffin road which runs westward from Broulin (Glen Strath Farrar) to Kintail. It starts from the head keeper's house at Inchvuilt and goes west up the Uisge Misgeach on what is now a well-made shooting path. About 3½ miles from Inchvuilt it turns up to the Bealach between Meallan Odhar and Beinn Dubh an Iaruinn. The path now fades away, but it is fair going north-west down to Aultfearn on the march burn near the shore of Loch Monar. The remains of a 'watcher's' house (Cosac) built during Mr Winan's tenancy over fifty years ago are seen on a small plot of green ground. Close by – roughly 200 yards south – are the ruins of old Jamie MacRae's smuggling bothies. It was here that Jamie's father, Alastair Mor na Pait, was caught by the *Gaugers* and taken prisoner to Inverness. Jamie and his father were famous old smugglers and did a good trade in the district. The story is told that for a while the proprietor, Captain Stirling of Fairburn, just winked at Jamie's trade, but when the thing got too notorious he felt he had to do something about it. So he made a pact with Jamie that if he would stop his smuggling the laird would see to it that it would be made up to him in other ways. Jamie agreed and kept loyally to his bargain; he dismantled his bothies and buried his still. The Government offers a reward of £5 for information which will lead to the capture of a still. Jamie was aware of this, and, when down at Beauly Market some time after, let it be known to the excisemen that he might be able to help them to discover a still, if the reward was forthcoming. So up came a posse of excisemen to Patt, and Jamie solemnly led them to a peat hole and pulled up his own copper pot and received £5 for his pains! I well remember old Jamie and his sister Mary forty years ago. They lived in their old thatched croft near the Patt Lodge jetty on Loch Monar. They left Patt a few years before their death, at Kilmorack, and their remains were taken (they were Kintail people) via Glen Convinth, Glen Moriston, and Glen Shiel to Kintail Churchyard, but the coffins of their father and mother were carried from Patt to Kintail Churchyard via Coire nan Each, Carnach, Killilan, and boat on Loch Long. The late Kenneth McLellan, who was keeper at East Monar, once told me that he was one of the company who carried Jamie MacRae's mother's coffin from Patt to Kintail. When they reached Carnach they were met by the Loch Alsh men, who relieved them of their long carry. "We were very tired when we got there," Kenneth remarked to me; "she was a big heavy woman too!"

From Patt the coffin road and right-of-way goes by the south side of An Gead Loch and up the Allt Coire nan Each, down by Loch Mhoicean, and on to Carnach.

A mile and a half north-east of Carnach there is a 'private' motor road down to Killilan, but foot passengers and droves and coffins use it as it is on the line of the old right-of-way. At Carnach the direct route to Kintail fords the river and goes south-west by the east shoulder of Meall Scouman, crossing the river at a point just above the Falls of Glomach, then over the Bealach na Sroine and down to Dorusduain.

A very touching little tale was told me some years ago by the head keeper of Broulin, Mr Peter Macdonald. His fellow-keeper was a man Campbell at Deanie in Glen Strath Farrar, and he lost his baby boy. Campbell was a Kintail man and the body of his wee boy had to be taken to Kintail. So he and Peter started off from Deanie by the route I have described by Inchvuilt, Patt, Coire Each, and Carnach. The story is now best told in Peter's own words: "We came to cross the river above the Falls of Glomach. I had never seen the falls before. I had the coffin under my arm, but I thought the wee fellow in it would not mind, and so I dropped down the hillside for a few hundred feet to where I could see the falls and 'we' had a good look and then went on our way to Kintail."

I expect it will be news to many people that Cromwell's General Monck in 1654 went westwards this way to overawe the clans. He commanded a force of horse and foot which included his own regiment, now the famous Coldstream Guards. This was a very daring enterprise in these days. He started from Perth and went by Aberfeldy to Kingussie, then across by Loch Laggan and Loch Lochy to Loch Quoich. From here he crossed over to Kintail by what must have been the Bealach Duibh Leac. Thereafter he went north by Glen Elchaig and Coire Each to the swampy ground near the Allt an Loin Fhiodha – just south of Loch an Gobhlach. In his dispatch he calls this camp 'Glen-teuch,' which is his English attempt at the pronunciation of the original Gaelic! Here are his own words: "29th July – I came to Glen-teuch in the Shields of Kintail, the night was very tempestuous and blew down most of the tents. In all this march we saw only two women of the inhabitants and one man. The 30th – The Army march't from Glen-teuch to Brouling. The way for neere 5 miles soe boggie that about 100 baggage horses were left behinde and many other horses bogg'd or tir'd. Never any horse men (much less an armie) were observed to march that way" (vide 'Transactions of the Gaelic Society of Inverness,' Vol. 18, p.70 and following).

Attadale
Attadale and North Kintail are little-known and seldom-traversed regions except by local sportsmen. But there are several old routes and rights-of-way through them, and it is right that they be here recorded.

Bendronaig Lodge is a sort of meeting-place for many of them. It should be noted that this Lodge is often only occupied in the shooting season so that pedestrians cannot count on rest and refreshment in spring or early summer. Make sure beforehand what the situation is.

From Bendronaig Lodge a right-of-way runs north by the east side of Loch an Laoigh through the Bealach Bhearnais and connects up west of Glenuaig Lodge with the routes to Strathconon. Also a right-of-way lies through the Bealach Sgoltaidh to Loch Monar. When the Dingwall and Skye Railway was first planned, it was up Glen Strath Farrar and through this Bealach that the line was to have been taken and not by Garve and

Achnasheen.

There is a private road from Bendronaig Lodge westwards to Attadale House; the right-of-way path is by the Bealach Alltan Ruairidh with a branch going north-west to Achintee, half a mile to the west of Lochan Fuara.

Eastwards from the Lodge a right-of-way goes by the north shore of Loch Calavie and An Gead Loch to Patt and southwards down the west bank of the River Ling to Killilan. A private motor road runs up the east bank of the Ling from Killilan to Coire Domhain and stops there. From Killilan also a right-of-way runs by Nonach Lodge to Attadale.

Glenelg to Glen Garry and Lochaber

In the old days sheep and cattle were ferried, or swam at slack tides, across Kylerhea from Skye to the mainland at Glenelg. What route did they then take to the southern markets? I feel pretty confident from personal acquaintance with the ground that it was by the Bealach Aoidhdailean (approximate pronunciation *oi-che-lun*). The Bernera Barracks were erected in 1722, and doubtless they were staffed and supplied by sea. I have examined an old military map in the British Museum (K. XLVIII. 62) by Daniel Paterson, dated 1746. In it a track is shown over the Mam Ratachan with the zigzags duly marked, proving that at that date there must have been a horse track to Kintail and up Glen Shiel. The road for wheeled traffic from Bernera to Fort Augustus was not made till 1775. When Boswell and Johnson passed through Glen Moriston on their way to Skye – 31st August 1773 – a party of soldiers were working on it.

The direct and easier route, however, for droves to the south would be by the Bealach Aoidhdailean to Kinloch Hourn and Glen Garry. This is a good track all the way, and it can be confidently recommended as a splendid cross-country walk.

There is a fair motor road through Glen Elg and up Glen Beag, which fades out as a road a mile or so beyond Balvraid. Thereafter it is a good horse track to Ruighe na Corpaich where you turn southwards up the Allt Ghleann Aoidhdailean to the Bealach. Over the summit the track is not at all distinct, but it is all good hard ground, and the track again becomes clear down the Allt an Tomain Odhar and on past Lochan Torr a' Choit through a narrow pass and then steeply down to Kinloch Hourn. Here the public road is joined. In the old days the droves would go to Greenfield practically along the line of the present road, fording the River Garry just west of Loch Garry.

From Greenfield there is a right-of-way south by Fedden and down Glen Cia-aig to Loch Arkaig. But the most frequented route would be eastwards from Greenfield for 2 miles and then up the east bank of the Ladaidh Burn and through by the north slopes of Ben Tee to Kilfinnan. Here is a very old and formerly much-used graveyard. The Glengarry Chiefs are buried here, and burial or memorial cairns where the coffin was rested can be seen here and there along the route.

At Kilfinnan there was easy access to the farther shore of Loch Lochy. (Before the canal was made it was dry ground here.) The droves would then go south by Letterfinlay to Lochaber or, alternatively, up Glen Gloy to Brae Roy and on to join the Corrieyairack road at Meallgarbha. This is still known as 'the soft road for the hoggs.' From Kilfinnan a good path runs along the west shore of Loch Lochy to the 'Dark Mile' at Achnacarry. This was the path Prince Charlie took when making for safety and France, two days after Culloden – April 1746.

I must not forget to record here a very important branch north from Quoich Bridge up Glen Quoich to Alltbeithe and then north-west over the Bealach Duibh Leac and down to Glen Shiel.

This was the route General Monck and his army used in July 1654. It is a coffin road also. Cairns may be seen at the side of the track in Wester Glen Quoich. On the Bealach itself, where there is a massive county stone dyke, a wide slap in the dyke has been made to let the droves and horses through. The track down the Allt Mhalagain is pretty steep at first just below the summit but perfectly feasible for cattle and horses, let alone sheep and humans.

It was over this pass that Prince Charlie and his party, six in all, travelled in July 1746. They had managed to slip through the line of sentries posted to intercept them in Coire Hoo. Reaching Coire Sgoir-adail they spent the day in 'a bit of hollow ground covered with long heather and branches of young birch bushes' in full view of the soldiers encamped at the head of Loch Hourn. Setting out that night they stumbled up Coire Sgoir-adail in pitch darkness and over the Bealach Duibh Leac down to Malagan in Glen Shiel, where they found shelter for the day behind a great boulder on the north bank of the river, about a mile east of Achnagart. This boulder is well known to the local inhabitants, and it is pointed out as 'Prince Charlie's Stone.'

Farther down Glen Garry there is an interesting old cut across from Glen Garry to Glen Moriston. It is a coffin road and used as such until recently.

The route starts from a place called Seanna-bhaile (old ground) about a mile west from Invergarry Bridge, and it goes more or less straight to Loch Lundie and on to near the top of Ceann a Mhaim where the coffin was rested, refreshments partaken of, and a cairn built. A number of the cairns are still seen.

The route then went over the east shoulder of the hill and down to Achlean in Glen Moriston. The graveyard is on the opposite side of the river, and there is a ford below the farmhouse quite close to the churchyard.

Here is a quaint tale told me by a Glen Moriston man. His uncle was staying at Invergarry when something went wrong with his leg and he had to have it amputated. His brother came across and carried the leg over Ceann a Mhaim and buried it in the old graveyard where they would all one day rest. This was forty-six years ago and shows what store the old Highlanders laid on their being buried, as far as possible, whole and intact, so that at the resurrection they would arise perfect and entire.

Kintail to Glen Cannich and Glen Affric*
There are two well-used passes from Kintail to the east – one by Glen Cannich and the other by Glen Affric.

The right-of-way to Cannich starts from 'The Iron Lodge' two miles north-east from Carnach in Glen Elchaig. It turns up east by a rough track and, passing Loch an Droma on the right, crosses the main watershed of the Atlantic and North Sea and goes on to Lungard, a keeper's cottage at present empty. In the old days the route kept along the north side of Loch Lungard past An Mam to the west end of Loch

* Parts of this route and some of the buildings mentioned now lie under the much-increased waters of Loch Mullardoch (which includes Loch Lungard – no longer named on current maps). 1993

Mullardoch at Coire-na-Cuillan.

There are still traces of one or two ruined houses to be seen along this route, but it is never used now, as a far easier and better way is to cross the river below Lungard by ford. A good shooting path is now struck which takes you easily to Ben Ula Lodge and then down the motor road past Cosac to Invercannich in Strath Glass. This road is a public one from Strath Glass as far as Liatrie, but thereafter it is kept up by the proprietors, and motors are accordingly not allowed on it except by permission. This is usually readily given except in the shooting season. There is no restriction to pedestrians; it is a right-of-way through to Kintail.

The other well-known pass from west to east is via Glen Affric, starting from Morvich at the head of Loch Duich.

This pass is undoubtedly one of the most ancient and much-frequented routes from west to east. St Duthac, an Irish saint and missionary, away back in the eleventh century, must often have used this route, travelling from Ireland to his shrine and church at Tain in Easter Ross. Loch Duich is St Duthac's Loch. The Bealach an Sgairne is also locally known as the Cadha Dhuich, which in Gaelic means St Duthac's Pass. A fine well near the top on the east side is called Topar Dhuich, St Duthac's Well.

From Morvich you go east for three-quarters of a mile and there cross the River Croe to Innis a' Chro'. You are apt to lose the track about here, but if you keep on north up the side of the burn you are sure to hit it, and thereafter it becomes a perfectly clear path up Gleann Choinneachain and through the Bealach an Sgairne, then down past the south end of Loch a' Bhealaich to the county march. The track about here

becomes rather indistinct, but just keep on down the north bank of the Allt Gleann Griomhaidh where the track again becomes quite good, and in another mile or so you are at Alltbeath, a hospitable keeper's house. From here it is plain and easy going down the north side of Loch Affric to Affric Lodge. Two miles farther on you reach the public road.

There is an alternative route from Morvich by the River Croe and Gleann Lichd and thence by the Allt Granda past Camban (now a deserted ruin) and so to Alltbeath. This route is perfectly feasible, but it is pretty rocky and steep going up the Allt Granda. The way over the Bealach an Sgairne is the historic one, and on the whole the easier.

The old and original route from Strath Glass to the west coast started from Tomich and went by Knockfin and across the slopes of Beinn nan Sparra, passing Loch an Eang, Loch a' Chlaidheimh, and Loch Pollan Buidhe on the left. It then crossed the Allt Garbh, where may be seen the ruins of an old change-house, and going west by what is now an excellent shooting path giving wonderful views to the north of Mam Sodhail and Loch Affric, it reached Athnamulloch. Here the River Affric was forded and Alltbeath reached some three miles farther on.

This route is now seldom used, the customary way now being through the Chisholm's Pass at Fasnakyle and along the north shore of Loch Benevian and the north shore of Loch Affric. The old route, as may be observed, kept on the south side of these lochs and joined the newer route beyond Athnamulloch at the west end of Loch Affric. There is a bit for about two miles west of Loch a' Chlaidheimh which is very rough going indeed, the old track, from disuse, being

76

overgrown with rank old heather. The route on the north side is all very good going. But it is right that the Knockfin Pass should be known about and occasionally used.

Athnamulloch (the ford of the Mull men) was the scene of a skirmish in 1721. After the Rebellion of 1715 the Estates of Seaforth, The Chisholm, and Grant of Glenmoriston were forfeited to the Crown, Estate Commissioners being appointed to collect the rents on behalf of the Crown. Donald Murchison, Seaforth's Chamberlain, ignored the forfeiture and continued to collect the rents and send them to the Earl on the Continent. The Chisholm and the Laird of Glenmoriston also continued to obtain their old patrimonies.

In 1721 more effective measures were decided on. On 13th September two Ross-shire Whigs, William Ross of Easter Fearn, and his brother, Robert Ross, a Bailie of Tain, under the escort of Lieutenant John Allardyce and a company of the Royal Regiment of the North British Fusiliers started from Inverness, passed through Glen Urquhart, and reached Glen Moriston. Thereafter they proceeded to Strath Glass and then prepared to make their way to Kintail by Glen Affric. Patrick Grant, Glenmoriston's second son, a lad of eighteen, who had watched these proceedings at Invermoriston, took the short route to Kintail and informed Donald Murchison of their intention to visit Kintail. Donald, who had some military experience as an officer in the Jacobite Army in 1715, determined to oppose them, and with about three hundred men crossed the hills towards Strath Glass.

They met at Athnamulloch on 2nd October, and after an exchange of fire Murchison and Easter Fearn had a parley, with the result that the factors retraced their steps. In the skirmish, Easter Fearn and his son Walter and several others were wounded. Walter's injuries proved fatal, and his body was carried by the Fusiliers via Wester Knockfin to Beauly and buried in the old Priory (vide *'Gaelic Society of Inverness Transactions,' Vol. 19, p.1 and following*).

The above account is largely quoted from Mr Mackay's paper.

Affric Lodge is one of the most beautifully situated lodges in the Highlands. It was built by the first Lord Tweedmouth in 1870, and shortly thereafter a sort of gentleman's agreement was come to providing that, if the old right-of-way via Knockfin and Sparra and the south side of Loch Affric was left unfrequented in order to give privacy to that side of the forest, Lord Tweedmouth would construct a good path along the north side and give the public wayleave over it. This was done, and both the proprietor and the public got the benefit.

When traversing these paths in this, and indeed in all deer-forest ground in August and September, don't make detours up the hillside; it's not fair to the shooting tenants, for you may spoil their dearly bought sport for days. So long as you are on the path, the deer will just stand and look at you. The moment you leave the path they're off 'over the hills and far away' and the sportsman may not see them again for weeks.

I remember the head keeper at Affric Lodge telling me how one year, just before the shooting began and before the then tenant, Lord Furness, had come north, he was watching and nursing a nice little parcel of good stags which had settled down in a corrie which runs up towards Mam Sodhail, just off the right-of-way path.

One morning he was out and about the lodge when three walkers came up and proceeded along the right-of-way path. He spoke to them and gave them information as to their way to the west coast, when one of them said, "Oh, but we are going to branch off in 3 miles up the corrie and climb Mam Sodhail." "Well, gentlemen," said the keeper, "may I ask you not to do that. I'm expecting Lord Furness to-morrow for the shooting. I have some nice stags up that corrie which I want him to see and later on to have a shot at. If you go up there to-day they will vanish, and I'll be blamed for having no stags on my beat. If you'll come back again when we're not shooting I'll do everything I can to help you, and I'll give you a day's fishing on Loch Affric as well!" The walkers were, I am glad to say, decent fellows and saw his point, and they gave up their climb and stuck to the path, and later on they came back and climbed their hill and had a splendid day's fishing in addition! This story, I think, shows the right way to go about the 'trespassing' difficulty, alike from the keeper's and from the walker's point of view.

Lochaber to Rannoch

I will now describe the old drove roads in Lochaber going to Rannoch and Argyllshire. Wade's High Bridge over the River Spean was the rallying point.

It was made about 1727, and before that date the ford at Dalnabea just below Corriecoillie would be the crossing used. It was this ford that Montrose used in his historic pounce on Argll's forces at Inverlochy.

The Marquis was at Aberchalder when Ian Lom, the Keppoch Bard, arrived hot-foot to give the news that Argyll with a force of 3,000 men was at Inverlochy threatening his rear. With characteristic swiftness Montrose determined to surprise him. Turning south up the Allt Chalder and over by the head-waters of the Turret into Brae Roy, he hurried down Glen Roy to Achavady, where he camped for the night. Next day he sped on through Bohontine and crossed the Spean at Dalnabea by a ford below Corriecoillie. He then took the backroad (to avoid observation) by Kylliehonnet, Lianachan, and Tomnafet. He came into the open at Torlundy and fell upon Argyll's outposts, who never dreamed that Montrose would have been able to bring armed forces that way. The next day – 2nd February 1645 – the Battle of Inverlochy was fought and Argyll and his forces routed, the Duke escaping by sea.

Starting from Fort William the great drove road southwards went by Spean Bridge and then by the south side of the River Spean, past Kylliehonnet and Corriecoillie and up the Larig between Cruach Innse and Stob Coire na Ceannain.

There is a road, just practicable for motors, which goes to a bothy about a mile beyond the summit of the pass. One has to be careful when on foot not to go as far as this bothy but to go through the gate in a sheep fence to the east, near the summit, and keep down the rough track on the south-west slopes of Stob Coire Easain. This takes one to Creaguaineach at the head of Loch Treig. From here the droves went south up Gleann Iolairean and down the Ciaran water to Ciaran, which was an old change-house and drove stance between Lochan Inbhir and Lochan-na-Salach Uidhre. These two lochs are now merged in the Kinlochleven Reservoir and Ciaran is under the waters. From Ciaran the droves went south by the Allt nam Fuaran and down to Kingshouse in Glencoe by the Allt Chailleach. At Kingshouse they struck the old military road which took them to Tyndrum and the south.

From Ciaran there was a branch eastwards up the Black Water and over the Bealach Triadan at Lochan a' Chlaidheimh where the three counties of Perth, Argyll, and Inverness meet; thereafter a junction would be made with the 'Road to the Isles' near the ford on the Allt Eigheach. This route from Fort William was the one most frequently used; it was easy going and afforded grazing *en route*.

The alternative route was along the old military road by Blarmachfoldach to Kinlochleven and over the Devil's Staircase to Kingshouse. This was much rougher and steeper and not so suitable for droves as the Larig route. At Lairigmor on the military road there was a drove road south to Callert on Loch Leven. Here was a ferry which took you across to Invercoe. This ferry has long been discontinued.

From Loch Treig head there is a fine right-of-way through to Glen Nevis by Steall. Formerly it was a poor track, but now it is much clearer and better owing to the use made of it by members of the Youth Hostels' Association travelling between the Hostels of Loch Ossian and Glen Nevis.

From Loch Treig head eastwards the drove road went steeply up the pass, crossing the Allt Luib Ruairidh just close to the railway. Here may be seen the ruins of an old house, probably a change-house and stance. The track then went east, skirting the west shores of Loch Ossian, and then along by the south side of the loch rising over the slopes of Meall na Lice, and on to old Corrour Lodge. This is now a roofless ruin, having been demolished after the building of the new lodge at the east end of Loch Ossian in 1897. (The Fort William railway was opened in August 1894.) From the

old lodge the route goes on south-east, a clear and distinct track, fording the Allt Eigheach and coming out on the main road half a mile east of Doire na-h Innis. This route just described is the 'Road to the Isles' and is a well-established right-of-way.

From Doire na-h Innis the droves, if eastward bound, would go down the road past Loch Eigheach and Dunan to Camusericht, then along the north side of Loch Rannoch. The drove route north from Loch Rannoch strikes off at Annet and goes north to Duinish, then along the west shore of Loch Garry to Dalnaspidal.

From Rannoch Station, a mile west of Doire na-h Innis (which was an old stance in existence long before the railway was made), a right-of-way goes through by the north side of Loch Laidon to Kingshouse. The track, which is pretty rough and uncertain, keeps by the loch side for about 1½ miles, and then slopes upwards, and passing above Tigh na Cruaiche (an old shepherd's house now a ruin) goes on west to the Black Corries Lodge. Here a motor road is picked up and the way is plain to Kingshouse. Coming in the reverse direction one has to be careful not to hold to the good path east of the lodge too long. This path leads down into the moor. At or about the Allt Dubh Mor you will see some small cairns leading eastwards; forsake the path and follow the cairns as best you can. As an old keeper once said to me, "You're not to keep to the path here, it will take you clean off the road!"

Rannoch to Gorton and Argyllshire

From the Braes of Rannoch the great outgate to Argyllshire started at Invercomrie and went up the west side of the Allt Chomraidh to the Grunnd nan Darachan. A private motor road has been made substantially along the line of the old drove road from Invercomrie to the Grunnd, and this bit is 'private' as far as motors are concerned, but a right-of-way for pedestrians and droves. From the Grunnd you go through the gate in the sheep fence and on south-west to the 'Shielings,' a cluster of ruined houses beside the Allt Beathe Beag at a height of about 1,200 feet. From here you follow through the heather, but quite easy going, south-west, keeping the same height till you come to 'The Clach' or the Rocking Stone. It is a group of granite Erratics piled on top of each other, and forms a remarkable feature, like the Sphinx in the desert, and a well-known rendezvous. It is about half a mile south-east of the Allt an Fhail, 1,200 feet above sea-level.

It should be noted that there is now no track hereabouts. Until about thirty years ago thousands of sheep went through here in September from Argyllshire to the wintering in Morayshire and back again in spring, and in these days the hoofmarks made the way distinct. To-day, owing to motor transport, the sheep are hardly ever taken through the moor, and the heather and the grass are supreme, but it is a well-established right-of-way and a valuable cross-country route for experienced hill-walkers. From 'The Clach' the way goes on keeping the same height and direction till you come to the march fence; here, at the point marked 1,228 feet on the O.S. map there is a gate to let the sheep and cattle through. Soon you reach the ruins of one or two shepherd's houses ('the caim hirsel').

Thereafter there is rather a boggy stretch to where the railway crosses the Water of Tulla. Under the railway and beside the water is a wide concrete passage, made to afford an easy passage for the beasts. The drove road then goes on down the riverside to Gorton, a shepherd's house (occupied and hospitable). From here there is a cart track down to Barravurich and past Achallader Farm, which joins the new Glencoe road at Loch Tulla.

Beside the new, comfortable little hotel at Bridge of Orchy there is a shepherd's house. 'The stance cottage' it is called, and the Achallader farmer is under obligation to allow night quarters for the droves and the men passing the stance.

From Bridge of Orchy the droves went down Glen Orchy to Loch Awe.

On the 'Road to the Isles' between Dunan and Loch Eigheach there was a connection south joining up with the Invercomrie-Gorton track near Grunnd nan Darachan.

It crossed the River Gaur by a ford just above 'Collie's Pool' below Loch Eigheach, and went up the west side of Gleann Duibhe to the Grunnd.

The 'soldiers' trenches' beside the railway some 3 miles west of the Grunnd are not trenches in the strict sense at all. They are an attempt at land reclamation on the part of Ensign James Small, the Government factor of the forfeited estate of Strowan Robertson. In 1763-64 he caused five great drains to be cut by soldier labour near where the Rannoch folk had their summer shielings, in an endeavour to sweeten up the ground, in the hope that crops might be made to grow there, but the experiment was not a success. These abandoned 'lazy beds' were for long an object of speculation, but I chanced on the explanation a few years ago (vide *Scottish History Society, 'Fortified Estate Papers,' p. 236*).

The pass leading south into Glen Lyon from Gorton was in the old days a very important and much-used route. Caterans and raiders, drovers and packmen,

Prince Charlie's men and the Hanoverian troops, all passed to and fro through this defile. The route struck off the Invercomrie-Gorton passage at 'the caim hirsel' and went south to the Allt Learg Mhearan and down to Invermeran in Glen Lyon – easy ground and good going if you keep up on the hillside a little, avoiding the boggy flats. It crossed the River Lyon at a ford at Lubreoch 3 miles down from Invermeran, then south up the Larig nan Lunn and down the Allt Truchill to Kenknock in Glen Lochay and so to Killin. This route is still used. There is a huge cairn at the summit of the Larig and guiding cairns here and there on the track.

It may be of interest to record that Thomas Telford, the great road and bridge maker, in 1810, put forward a proposal to the Commissioners for Highland Roads and Bridges that a road be constructed from Tulloch in Glen Spean to Killin. It was to cost £15,360; but the proposal was never carried out owing to 'local' indifference. The road was to have started at Tulloch, held along the east shore of Loch Treig and up into the Moor of Rannoch at Corrour; it was then to have run south and, crossing the River Gaur just east of Loch Laidon, would have gone right through the moor, practically following the line of the West Highland Railway to Gorton, then through the pass to Invermeran in Glen Lyon, up into Glen Lochay by the Larig, and down Glen Lochay to Killin.

Had this proposal of Telford's been carried out it would have been a wonderful road, opening up the country seventy years before the railway did so (vide *'Fifth Report of the Commissioners for Roads and Bridges in the Highlands of Scotland.' Printed April 1811. All these Reports contain much valuable information to those who are interested in this subject*).

The Highland Military Patrols after 1745

After the Rising of 1745 the Highlands remained for several years in a very unsettled state and the Hanoverian Government took steps to control the situation. They established in various parts of the north a series of military posts to watch the Highlanders, that there should be no chance of their gathering together again, to put a stop to cattle raiding, and to enforce the Disarming Act which forbade all carrying of arms and the wearing of the Highland dress.

In the north-west Highlands, the district which I have dealt with, there was a Captain's Command at Laggan Achadrom, between Loch Lochy and Loch Oich, and another at the west end of Loch Rannoch at Invercomrie (the shooting lodge there still bears the name of 'The Barracks').

At Laggan Achadrom (the headquarters) there were a captain, a sergeant, a corporal, and ten men. There were ten outlying posts, each having a non-commissioned officer and five to eight men; also a moving patrol of a lieutenant, a sergeant, a corporal, and twenty men.

These posts were established at:

1. The head of Glan Moriston.
2. Knockfin.
3. Strath Cluny.
4. Head of Glen Shiel.
5. On the Bealach between Loch Garry and Loch Quoich.
6. Garvamore in the Corrieyairack.
7. Leichroy at the head of Glen Roy.
8. Head of Glen Spean.
9. High Bridge.
10. Nine Mile Bridge (at foot of Glen Gloy).

As constant communication must have been kept up between these posts and their headquarters it meant that many of the routes described in this article must have been constantly used by the soldiers going to and fro with prisoners, information, and supplies.

Here is an extract of the patrolling officer's report:

Places visited (from Laggan Achadrom).
June 6, 1749. Station between Loch Garry and Quoich.
June 7, 1749. Glen Shiel.
June 8, 1749. Strath Cluny.
June 8, 1749. Head of Glen Moriston.
June 9, 1749. Knockfin.
June 9-10, 1749. Fort Augustus.
June 11, 1749. Garvamore and Garvabeg.
June 12, 1749. Glen Spean.
June 12, 1749. Leichroy.
June 12, 1749. Nine Mile Bridge.
June 12, 1749. High Bridge.

Reading between the lines of the above itinerary the patrol travelled from Laggan Achadrom past Invergarry and up along the side of Loch Garry and Loch Quoich.

Turning north up Glen Quoich it must have crossed over the Bealach Duibh Leac and down into Glen Shiel, then up to Strath Cluny and down Glen Moriston. From Torgyle over by Loch na Beinn Baine to Knockfin (near Tomich); back by the same way and across to Fort Augustus; over the Corrieyairack to Garvamore and westwards to Glen Spean; up Glen Roy to Leichroy and then through the Glen Gloy and down to Nine Mile Bridge (still fresh and intact near Glen Fintaig Farm), down Wade's road to High Bridge and back by the same way to Laggan Achadrom.

The officer in charge of the moving patrol would almost certainly be on horseback, so the routes involved must in 1749 have been practicable for horses and not mainly foot tracks, which is interesting.

Another important centre was at Invercomrie, Loch Rannoch. Here were stationed a captain, a sergeant, a corporal, and eight men.

There were outlying posts, each having a non-commissioned officer and four to six men; also a moving patrol of a lieutenant, two sergeants, a corporal, and twenty-one men. These posts were established at:

1. The head of Loch Leven.
2. The head of Glencoe.
3. Derrybeg (on the north side of the Tulla Water at Achallader).
4. The Bridge of Kinnachan (Tummel Bridge).
5. Dalnacardoch.
6. Inderchadden.
7. The head of Glen Lyon (Invermeran).

Here is a report in the actual words of the officer commanding, Captain Patten of General Guise's Regiment:

"June 15, 1750. I visited all the Posts within my district from Invercomery by Slis Mine (*i.e.*, the north side of Loch Rannoch) and Laudakin (?) to Dalnacardock. From Dalnacardock across the Bridge of Innesour (Trinafour) to the Bridge of Kinnachan (Tummel Bridge). From Kinnachan through the wood along the River Tumble to Inderchadden. From Inderchadden by Cary in Slis Garrow (south side of Loch Rannoch) to Glen Lion head. From Glen Lion head by Golaviran (Gorton) to Derry Begg (Achallader). From Derry Begg by Loch Ball (Baa) and Glen Esky (Etive) to Glencoe head. From Glencoe head across the Ferry on Loch Leven (at Callert) and up to the head of the Lochs.

"From Loch Leven head by Loch Erach (Eigheach) across the Tickek-a-Doughe which divides Perth, Argyle, and Inverness-shire to Invercomery."

Here too, reading between the lines, we can picture the officer on horseback and his twenty-one weary men making their way from Invercomery down the north side of Loch Rannoch to Annet and then up and over by Loch Garry to Dalnacardoch; from Dalnacardoch they would come back by Wade's road to Tummel Bridge, then turning west they reached Inderchadden at Kinloch Rannoch. Their route would now be by the south side of Loch Rannoch past Carie to Dall and over the 'Kirk Road' to Innerwick in Glen Lyon and up Glen Lyon to Invermeran; then through the Caim Pass to Gorton and down to Derrybeg over against Achallader. From Derrybeg they must have cut through to Loch Baa and the top of Glen Etive to Glencoe head. This post would probably be somewhere near Altnafeadh. Down Glencoe and across the ferry to Callert and up

the north side of Loch Leven to its head and on to Ciaran. From Ciaran they would travel up the Black Water and join the 'Road to the Isles,' following it down past Loch Eigheach to Invercomrie.

A great trek, and this done in 1750! Even to-day it would be some walk. But I imagine that in those far-off days the tracks across the moors would be even better than they are to-day. They would be more used then than now and this would make them harder, more distinct, and better going.

For a partial rescript of these Military Reports consult Allardyce's 'Historical Papers,' Vol. 2, p.513 and following. New Spalding Club, 1896. These Reports throw a vivid light on the condition of the Highlands after the Forty-five.

n.b. All AER's place-name spellings have been left unaltered.

A note on the slides

The Reverend Robertson took his first slide in 1903, after he had completed his Munros, and his last around 1935. Why he stopped, we do not know; possibly his plate camera simply gave up the ghost.

On his death, the glass slides were given to the S.M.C. collection, of which he himself had been custodian for a while before the First World War. They were latterly held on behalf of the Club by the late Graham Tiso. From the collection of thousands of slides, we initially chose a couple of hundred, narrowing these down to the 95 we have published. The criteria for selection were influenced by the following factors.

Initially we thought to reproduce the *Minister's Munros*, imagining he carried a camera with him on his peak-bagging rounds. But he did not, and huge areas of the Highlands he seldom, if ever, visited again after his completion in 1901. Thus there are almost no slides of the Cairngorms, or of the Northern Highlands, and few of the Southern or Central Highlands (using the geographical conventions of the S.M.C. Guide-books.) The vast majority of the slides were of the 'golden triangle' between the Great Glen, western seaboard, and the Inverness-Kyle railway line, with the addition of Skye, and a lesser Nevis-Glencoe salient. The selection of slides inevitably reflects this.

Then we tried to avoid using slides already in print, in favour of new ones; or at least to try and omit those included in other books currently in print, in favour of those from out-of-print works. Though some familiar slides, essential to the text, have been included, the great majority, to our knowledge, have not been published before – other than in pre-war SMC Journals and SMC guide-books long out of print.

Then, while trying to do credit to AER's camera skills, we wanted to avoid printing simply 'pretty pictures' – though some were so good, they had to be included! Our main intention was that the slides should say something about social changes in the Highlands, or about mountaineering cultural history. Occasionally this meant using a less glamourous slide which said more than a more photogenically stunning rival for inclusion – which may have left us, so to speak, 'speechless'. We are confident that the final selection will give the reader a taste of the excitement and satisfaction we experienced in researching AER's whole photographic opus.

AER's photographs often show, inadvertently, changes in the Scottish Highlands. These two slides of Kinloch Aylort, however, are certainly a deliberate record of change. They are taken at more than a quarter-century of an interval, from almost the identical spot. The first picture was one of Robertson's early slides, taken only 5 years after the railway to Mallaig had breached this area's isolation, and a car's appearance would have been a major event. (May, 1906)

The second picture was taken on a motoring holiday, at a time when the Road to the Isles had become popular with the private motorist and coach operators. Change is evident. In the place of four black houses, with thatched roofs, we have a sad series of ruins, and a new white house with corrugated iron roof as the only remaining habitation. The fields are also less tended, dykes decayed and cultivated areas reverted to rough grazing. Kinloch Aylort mirrors massive depopulation everywhere in this period in the Highlands. (Apr. 1933)

AER in Skye 1899.

An interesting portrait of the Munroist at the height of his pilgrimage. Robertson was in Skye with the Inglis Clarks, and this photograph was taken by William Inglis Clark. We could point out the hemp rope, nailed boots and the fob watch, but more interesting is the general demeanour of AER. Far from the stiff Victorian image presented in slides by many other pioneers, Robertson here appears as a rather gallus lad, hands behind the head and legs apart in a rather ungentlemanly fashion. Unbuttoned cuffs and a stray item of clothing offset his relaxed style. Possibly the prospect of matrimony, and of becoming a "compleat" man – in the sense of finishing his Munros, that is – were pleasing to him.

The Gendarme, 1905.
On subsequent trips to Skye, AER had
his own camera and took many
photographs. This one shows a climber
'embracing' the Gendarme on the south-
west ridge of Sgurr nan Gillean, watched
by his companion at a safe distance. Like
many others, Robertson recorded this
striking monolith, but it is too late to copy
his example; it collapsed in 1987, making
the ridge an easier prospect.

Mrs Chisolm's, Glenbrittle.

This undated slide is interesting, in that it records a house which was used from 1912 onwards by climbers as accommodation in the glen, before the Hostel and the BMC hut existed. It was also a Post Office, since there were several families at that time on the far side of the river, where today only ruins and holiday homes exist. There was a school also, to which the children in the slide would have gone. How seldom do those who throng to Glen Brittle now seem to cross the rickety bridge to the old settlement. The shed containing the P.O. is there yet.

The Cioch.
This was not one of AER's slides, but one gifted to him by Buchanan. It is surely one of the earliest photographs of the rock protuberance, though not the first, since Collie took a picture when he confirmed its existence, suspected by a shadow cast, in 1899.

What it shows is the virgin nature of the Cuillin at this time; hardly a boulder has been stirred or rock scratched on the way to the Cioch. And in Coire Lagan below, today criss-crossed by the paths of mountaineers' feet – not a single track!

Sgurr nan Gillean. When the first mountaineers came to the Cuillin the compass was unreliable–it still is, due to the gabbro rock–maps were worse, and the climbers revised the O.S. ones for their own use. And the hills were trackless: no stalkers' paths or cart-tracks here, as on much of the mainland. The doughty pioneer shown here, pointing the way to the summit of Sgurr nan Gillean, has taken the precaution of bringing a rope with him, possibly unsure of what to expect. He is following what is now the Tourist path, but there are no cairns – only huge amounts of loose rock – and no path! Behind him loom the towers of Pinnacle Ridge.

Pinnacle Ridge.

When Robertson started mountaineering, there were still summits in Skye which were unclimbed, and even when he visited the island for the first time in 1898 many of the plums of the ridge, such as King's Chimney and the Basteir Tooth, had only recently been done.

One such plum was Pinnacle Ridge, which AER completed with the Inglis Clarks in 1898. This is a straightforward scramble till the Third Pinnacle. From this a descent, either by climbing down, or abseiling, is necessary to the slanting ledge in the centre of the picture. This ledge is now much worn.

John Mackenzie.

In contemplative mood, we have John Mackenzie, the Cuillin guide, who was often hired by AER when the Reverend was in Skye. On occasion complaints were heard as to AER monopolising John, whose safe and skilled services were always in demand. Here he is looking towards Sgurr Alasdair, the highest Cuillin peak, with the Inaccessible Pinnacle – up which he led many a client – as the far excrescence.

A crofter from Sconser, Mackenzie guided for much of his life, but is most remembered for his partnership with the great mountaineer Norman Collie, with whom he recorded many first ascents.

Cuillin Camping.

On very few occasions did the Reverend camp, so it is worth recording this instance in the Fionn Coire. Though the ladies are dressed as if going for tea at Cranston's – and indeed there appears to be a picnic basket – there is also a rope, so some scrambling at least was envisaged. Possibly, however, given the small tent and four people, it was merely a picnic arrangement, for decorum's sake? Somewhere the ladies, who often climbed in breeches, could retire to don their obligatory skirts for the photograph as they poured the tea? The hill in the background is Bruach na Frithe, the easiest of the Munros of Skye to ascend. An easy day for a lady? (June, 1906)

Creag Meagaidh and
Ladhar Bheinn.
A fine pair of mountain
portraits which complement each other. The first is
of Creag Meagaidh, showing the three Posts clearly
as well as the Window. The former are the scene of
winter climbing, the latter of an episode in the Young
Pretender's wanderings, in which AER maintained a
keen interest.

What this shows, as does the slide of Ladhar Bheinn and Loch Hourn is the still moderately extensive tree cover in these areas, sadly since much reduced by over-grazing from sheep and deer due to short-sighted economic policies. Both peaks are regarded as amongst the finer in the Munroist's round. And thankfully, while the N.C.C. has acquired Meagaidh and is engaged in re-afforestation, the John Muir Trust had purchased Ladhar Bheinn to prevent misguided 'development'. (Ladhar Bheinn, June, 1926)

Monar.
These two photographs also record, unintentionally, historical change. The first shows the east end of Loch Monar, looking towards Maoile Lunndaidh, while the second shows Strathmore in west Monar, with Bidean a'Choire Sheasgaich (left) and Sgurr Choinnich (rt.) in the distance. These are three of the remotest Munros in Scotland, and all much prized by the legatees of the Reverend.

While the hills are still there, Strathmore is not, and has been flooded by the Monar Dam, which has raised the loch to drown a stalkers' path which used to follow the north side of the loch, and also some of the foreground forest. This area was much visited by AER, but the loss of many paths makes it harder going for today's walker.

Strathmore Cottage.

Another advantage AER had in Monar, was good accommodation. When Robertson visited Strathmore, one house open to him was Strathmore Cottage, shown here with Sgurr na Conbhaire and the ridge from Sgurr Choinnich to Sgurr a' Chaorachain in the background.

The house was occupied by a shepherd till flooded by the Monar dam in 1962.

The first slide shows carefully fenced off trees. These were planted for shelter, and always included a rowan, or rodden, to ward off evil spirits.

The second slide of Strathmore Dyre shows Sgurr na
Lapaich to the south, another very remote Munro. Note
the ground dyked and fenced off for cultivation. Indeed,
the last occupant grew and harvested hay till he left. In
AER's day it was occupied by a Keeper.

Jamie MacRae's, West Monar.
A classic black house, of unhewn stone with battened-down thatched roof, shared by Mairi and her brother Hamish Dhu (Jamie). The house was built by Alistair Mhor, their father, who squatted on an island in Loch Monar in the 1840s, (after coming from Kintail). Originally shared with animals, an adjacent byre was there by the time AER took this slide in the early twentieth century.

Beinn Fhada, 1906.
The Western Highlands remained probably AER's greatest love. Here we see a portrait of Beinn Fhada (Attow) a Munro in western Glen Affric. The picture is taken from near Alltbeithe, now a Youth Hostel, but then occupied, looking through towards Camban (another occupied house then, now an M.B.A. bothy) and Kintail.
Note the excellent condition of the road then, a functioning pony and trap thoroughfare, compared to now. And the amount of snow for May!

Bealach an Sgairne, 1906.
On this occasion, AER did not visit Camban, but walked between Beinn Fhada and A'Ghlas Bheinn, another Munro already 'bagged', on the high route to Kintail. The path looks well-maintained, and so too does the sheep fence in the picture.
His wife, Kate, with rucksack and decorous long skirt, offsets the composition.

Loch Arkaig, May 1906.
On the same holiday, Robertson and his wife headed for Knoydart. Here we see Kate posed by the loch, with the peaks of the Rough Bounds in the distance. Spring – note the trees – was late that year.

Kate's garb is interesting. Plenty of clothes, and a bit of bulk in the rucksack, but little heavy. No tent, little food, no cooking gear, since accommodation was always to hand. Note the good track.

Strathan, 1906.

One source of accommodation was the farm at Strathan, at the west end of Loch Arkaig. AER stayed here and at Glen Dessary a couple of miles further west. The view is towards Glen Pean, where there was also an occupied cottage open to visitors. Strathan is now a holiday home, as is Glen Dessary; Glen Pean is an M.B.A. bothy.

The mountainscape is of Streap, a magnificent peak, though no Munro, hence ignored by AER. To the right is Sgurr Thuilm which was high enough to be graced by the Reverend's feet. Note the sturdy bridge going towards Glen Pean, and the deer-proof protection round the fields by the house. Clearly, a functioning farm in 1906, as were several other habitations in the vicinity at that time. Now the whole area is swamped by private monocultural forestry operations, with no permanent inhabitants.

Glen Dessary, 1906.

Looking from Glen Dessary towards Garbh Chioch Mhor, a hill which only achieved Munro status in 1974, and which overlooks the Mam na Cloich Airde pass into the 'Rough Bounds' of Knoydart. The track today is in much the condition AER found it in 1906, except that in the interests of the omnipotent conifer, it has been bulldozed much further up the glen, now heavily wooded. The Mam na Cloich Airde must have been one of the last-used drove roads, as the Knoydart people still took their cattle over it to the road-end at Strathan in the 1930s.

The Five Sisters, 1930.
Another historical photograph. This unobscured view of the Five Sisters of Kintail was doubtless taken as a portrait of the ridge containing five Munros (Sgurr Fhuaran is the shapely, central peak), but records much more.

Now this view is obscured by monocultural forestry operations, and indeed the plantings can already be seen in the picture. Secondly the old Wade's road has been much 'improved' with the hairpin bends eliminated and a semi-motorway constructed, which bypasses the decaying historical bridges.

Liathach from Loch Clair.
Robertson does not appear to have visited Torridon as frequently as certain other West Highland areas, and the reason for his trip in the Spring of 1935 was for more than just to make a study of the finest of its hills in snowy mantle. (It was one of his last slides.)

At this time the right of way by Loch Clair and Loch Coulin via the Coulin Pass to Achnashellach was challenged by the estate. AER's researches and discussions with the factor convinced them to compromise, and concede a slightly altered right of way.

The Corrieyairack Pass, 1925.
A Wade's bridge that AER helped to save, through his work in the Rights of Way Society. Funds were made available to repair this bridge on the Corrieyairack Pass, and it is still in place.

The site of the bridge is Lagan a' Bhainne, or milky hollow, an old, verdant and sheltered grazing for cattle. It was the site of the camp of Redcoat sappers who built the road, and they called it Snugborough.

Bridge Builders, 1932.

Interestingly, when Rights of Way volunteers repaired the bridge, two centuries after its construction, they chose the same place for their encampment. And the design and reliability of tents had probably not come far since the eighteenth century either!

Sartorial styles are interesting. There are a couple of residual Empire-builders – the lad seated left looks like an Indian D.C. Some favour the para-military styles then popular in outdoor pursuits, echoing the uniformed political youth movements of the 1930s. And the lad standing second right has a proto-Yuppie smartness about his clothes and hairstyle. Comparing these styles with pre-first-war dress, shows the loosening of social attitudes, and the broadening of the social basis of outdoor pursuits, since 1914.

Glen Shiel, 1923 and 1931.
Two portraits, from different parts of the Glen, looking
towards the Saddle, the only Munro with an English
name, and the sharp prow on the left of Faochag.

The Reverend had improved his transport, from a motorbike and side-car in the first slide, to a car, seen by the road, in the second. The sheep-fank remains, as in 1923, but the thatched roof is gone; as is the house seen further down the glen. Now there is no habitation between Cluanie and Kintail.

Two Portraits from the Easter Meet, 1931.
By the early 1930s, though S.M.C. President, A.E.R. was less inclined to visit the tops on meets – he was over 60. But aside from conviviality, he enjoyed photographing the hills he had "compleated" 30 years before.

Aonach air Chrith is one of the peaks on the South Glenshiel Ridge, much prized by the Munroist, because the ridge contains seven Munros, of which this is one of the finer.

Spidean Mialach and Gleouraich (rt.) from the north. Probably taken as AER was descending the east ridge of Aonach air Chrith. At the time these two hills would have been more easily approached from Cluanie. The old road from the back of the inn then crossed the glen now occupied by the raised waters of Loch Loyne and continued over the hill to Tomdoun in Glen Garry. Relics still enjoyed by today's hill-walkers are the system of superbly constructed stalker's paths that sweep up to the tops from Loch Quoich and Altbeithe.

Beinn Dorain.
The classic view of the mountain, from what was the main road, but is now a part of the West Highland Way. Auch farm is now blanketed by a thick growth of trees.

Note the trodden path beside the road; were people frightened of walking on the road, or did the animals prefer the softness of the path?

Ben Achallader 1925.

A splendid portrait of a fine hill, highlighted by the spring snows. Visible is Crannach Wood, one of the largest remaining relics of the Caledonian Forest, still sadly unfenced and unregenerating today. Invisible as it passes through the wood is the West Highland railway – another endangered species.

En Route to Ben Lui, Easter 1905.
A group of climbers, early in the day. What is interesting is the attire. Apart from boots and gaiters, and one muffler, they could be off for a day in the office. Gear is also limited to an ice-axe each, and a small rucksack between four, aside from the last man's small pack. The snow seems in good condition, as they set off for Central Gully, a prized winter route in those days.

Ben Lui.
Safety first, on emerging from Central Gulley in winter. Two anchor men and a standing belay ensure minimum trepidation for the climber emerging from the cornice. The photograph is taken from near the summit, looking towards Stob Garbh. From these and other slides, it is doubtful if AER took part in the climb.

Two Studies of the Buachaille.
Taken in Spring and September 1928. The first is from near Blackrock Cottage, which still stood by the old road, seen clearly. The cottage was acquired for the LSCC, a process in which Winifred, AER's wife, was involved. Note there was a fenced, cultivated area round the cottage; apparently the ladies used to grow flowers in the garden. It was quieter then, without the road to the ski-tow which exists today.

A splendid study of the Kingshouse Inn, without the shanty-town spread which has attached itself there since. Note the extensive hay-cutting and the stooks in the foreground. In the background looms the mighty Buachaille, soon to be acquired by the National Trust for Scotland – due mainly to the legacy of Percy Unna – with the rest of Glencoe.

New Roads through the Glen. May 1930.
AER was obsessed by the building of the new Glencoe road, and took many slides of it. Here are two, the first of which shows rock cutting at the Study, high up in the glen, beside the Meeting of the Three Waters. Road-building had become mechanised, and other slides show steam-rollers and mechanical shovels. Here we see the bogies on a purpose-built miniature railway, to carry away the dross produced by the workers seen further up the line.

The second slide (April 1932) shows the new road in all its splendour, and a new bridge, where it joins the old – also with bridge – upriver from the Clachaig Inn. It also shows the Aonach Eagach, at the far end of which is the last of Robertson's Munros, Meall Dearg, which he had climbed 31 years before. Though he greeted the new road enthusiastically, I wonder what AER would think now of the many parking places which litter the glen? Some feel a parking ban, with shuttle bus would be an improvement; others that the road should be closed, dug up and re-routed.

122

Glencoe, 1928.
Gearr Aonach, one of the Three Sisters,
with part of Stob Coire an Lochain in the
background (rt.). Not a Munro, only a
top, though many would passionately
disagree with such a classification.
The house in the foreground is the only
habitation between Altnafeadh and
Achtriochtan, and was for a while
Hamish MacInnes' home. Here it stands
by the old road, now the new road gives it
a berth.

Schiehallion.
The 'Minister's Munro', since he could virtually see it from his manse at the Braes of Rannoch. This view is taken from further east, and shows a part of the Black Wood of Rannoch, another Caledonian relic.

Surprisingly, while at Rannoch, Robertson hardly climbed, adding instead to his preaching, that other pursuit of the man from Galilee, carpentry. Dated June 1923, this slide was taken on a nostalgic return journey to his former parish.

Rannoch Moor, 1925.
Looking south on a fine summer's day towards Beinn Achaladair and the adjacent hills, over the empty wastes of Rannoch Moor. Today the view is less empty, since much of the area has been planted with conifers.

Ironically the Soldiers' Trenches, from where the slide was taken were an early attempt to drain the moor for cultivation. The government took over Jacobite estates after the '45, and the Redcoats tried to improve the summer pastures on the moor.

Carn Mor Dearg.
A winter study of the north-west ridge leading to the summit of Carn Mor Dearg, one of Scotland's 4,000 ft peaks. It was climbed by AER as early as 1895, when he remarked on the narrowness of the arête continuing south and west to Ben Nevis. From it the finest views of the Nevis ridges and buttresses are gained.

North East Buttress, June 1924.
An attractive study of the great Nevis Ridge, in fine weather, but with much late snow, especially at the foot of the Orion Face. As he took the photograph, was AER musing about the time he had tried to descend the buttress in the company of Naismith, the great mountaineer and 'father' of the S.M.C. On that occasion the Reverend had got off-track, and the duo climbed back to the summit. Today the faces and gulleys of North-East Buttress are one of the Meccas of Scottish rock and snow and ice climbing.

C.I.C. Hut 1928.
Shown is a party at the building of the hut on Ben Nevis. Most of the materials would have been transported by ponies such as the one shown, and indeed coal for the hut was delivered by such methods till after the Second World War. The three workmen are accompanied by a gaffer-type, with stick and fob watch. He must have been pleased that they have the timber for the hut covered by a tarpaulin against the weather.

C.I.C. Interior, Sept. 1929.
Robertson was the Vice-President of the S.M.C. when the Nevis hut was under construction, and he played his part. As well as constructing a table for the hut – not shown in the slide but still in use today – he also officiated as chaplain at its opening. A further point was that the hut was erected in memory of Charles Inglis Clark, killed in the First World War. He was the son of AER's old friend of many years' standing, William Inglis Clark.

Poolewe 1905.
The Robertsons in tandem, so to speak. The sturdy velocipede, with panniers to carry equipment, but no gears, served them well on Highland roads before AER gained access to a car. Kate's mannish attire, with shirt and tie, contrasts with Robertson's natty bunnet and smart tweed suit. Already over 50, Kate must have had a strong constitution to undergo the rigours of long cycling and walking trips.

Ballachulish Ferry, Sept. 1929.

Even the advent of the motor-car did not take the adventure out of mountaineering. Here is how one such mountaineer described the process of negotiating the same ferry in July 1906. G. Bennet Gibbs investigated the charge (1 shilling per cart.) and screwed up courage to risk the car on an apparently inadequate boat.

Two stout planks are placed abeam, resting on the gunwales of the boat; the car is run down and turned crosswise on the slipway by lifting, and then pushed on to the planks which project over the stones from the boat alongside. In our case, the forewheels rested exactly above the one gunwale and the back wheels over the other, being chocked with wooden wedges, but not tied down at all. The state of the tide was favourable ... (SMCJ 9, p.12)

Kylesku Ferry.
A real hi-tech, roll-on, roll-off ferry by contrast, carrying a car and a dog which has come along for the ride – not to mention the wee boy. The boat in the background looks more like a fishing boat than a pleasure craft.

Index